Forgive

HEALING RELATIONSHIPS THROUGH FORGIVENESS

ACCEPTING GOD'S GRACE AND
GIVING IT TO OTHERS

A BOOK SHORT

DONALD E. JONES, PHD

J & A Book Publishers
www.jabookpublishers.com

ISBN-13: 978-0692741238
ISBN-10:0692741232

DEDICATION

I dedicate this book to my Savior and Lord Jesus Christ. He has been with me every step of my journey upon the earth, and I so look forward to being in His presence forever and ever.

CONTENTS

ACKNOWLEDGMENTS

I want to thank my wonderful and gracious wife Carol who has supported me in this ministry with sacrifice, enthusiasm, encouragement, and accountability. Most of all, she has been a constant blessing because of her willingness to listen. I was always sharing with her the truths God had been teaching me as I studied His word and wrote this book. It consumed many hours. Thank you, Carol and I deeply love you.

I want to thank my son Gregory R. Jones for volunteering to be the primary editor of this important book. Without his time and effort in painstakingly and meticulously going over every word and every sentence checking and rechecking the sentence structure and grammar, I would not have been able to complete it. Thank you for your ministry to me.

I want to thank my other children, Krista, Matt, and Kara for their love for Christ and His Word and their willingness to live for Him. I love you all.

Introduction

After Moses had received the Ten Commandments, the prophet and leader requested that God show him His glory. The Almighty explained to Moses that no human could see Him and live. Nevertheless, God would grant his request by allowing His servant Moses to experience the passing of His "goodness" by him and the actual viewing of the "backside of His glory." On the next morning, he stood upon a rock and called upon the name of the Lord. The Lord God descended in the form of a cloud, shielded Moses in the cleft of the rock, and covered him with His divine hand. As God displayed His divine glory visibly, He declared the many attributes of His supernatural, divine character.

In Exodus 34:6-7, Moses described this amazing moment, and the words that he heard the Lord declare about Himself, "Yahweh [I AM THAT I AM] passed by before him, and he proclaimed, 'Yahweh! Yahweh, a merciful and gracious God, slow to anger, and abundant in His loving kindness and truth, keeping loving kindness for thousands, forgiving iniquity and disobedience and sin'" (DEJ). A book written on healing relationships through forgiveness by its nature must begin with the proclamation that the God of the universe is not only a merciful, gracious, patient, loving, kind, truth-filled, just, and righteous God but the Almighty God who "forgives iniquity, transgressions, and sin." The Lord God announced that He is a "forgiving" God.

This by no means negates the fact that He is also a just and righteous one; therefore, this forgiveness comes with a price that had to be paid. So, He sent His Son to die to pay the penalty for our sins in order to pour out His forgiveness upon all mankind. Through faith in Jesus Christ, men and women experience the full extent of His forgiveness that was

1

proclaimed to Moses many years ago on that mountain top. Once this has occurred in our lives, we are to live for Him. We are to act like Him, and we are to obey Him. One of the critical ways in which God desires His forgiven people to live for, act like, and obey Him is *to forgive others as we are forgiven*. This is the key point of this book. As the Lord God has forgiven us and healed our relationship with Him, He requires us to forgive and heal our relationships with others. This is found in several critical passages in the Scriptures. Two of them are mentioned by our Lord and one from the apostle Paul. All three clearly explain the important truth that relationships are to be "reconciled" and "restored" to "gain back" one's brother, sister, or neighbor. This is done primarily through forgiveness.

In Matthew 5, the Lord Jesus discusses the heart attitudes people in His kingdom should possess. After speaking of anger, the Lord presents a general principle of living in His kingdom on earth. In verses 23-24, He explains, "If therefore you are offering your gift at the altar, and there remember that your brother has anything against you, leave your gift there before the altar, and go your way. First be reconciled to your brother, and then come and offer your gift." The Greek word translated "reconciled" means "to make changes." It originates from a Greek root word that was a banking term meaning "to render accounts the same." There would be a discrepancy between two bank ledgers, and all the mistakes would have to be found and corrected in order for them to agree. We express this between people as "being on the same page." The Lord indicates that the Father desires His people to come to Him fully reconciled with each other. If we, as Christians, know that someone harbors something against us, we are to take the initiative and go to them and reconcile with them. We should not wait for them to come to us. We take our responsibility and go to them. We must once again "settle accounts." They have the same responsibility.

In Matthew 18, Jesus discusses those who are sinning in the church and what all believers should do. In verse 15, the Lord commands, "If your brother sins against you, go, show him his fault between you and him alone. If he listens to you, you have gained back your brother." The Greek word translated "gain" refers "to obtaining or securing something." When a relationship is restored, we gain back everything that the other parties contributed. In this particular case, we have something against our brother, rather than the reverse. If this does happen, we are to take the initiative and confront our brother or sister to gain him or her back and restore the relationship. So, whether someone has something against us, or we have something against someone else, the procedure is essentially the same. Christians must take the initiative and reconcile with them.

The third passage involves the restoration of a sinning brother in the church. In Galatians 6, Paul opens the chapter with an explanation of how to help a sinning saint. In verse one, Paul asserts, "Brothers, even if a man is caught in some fault, you who are spiritual must restore such a one." The Greek word translated "restore" means "to render fit, sound, or complete; to mend or repair what has been broken." The word is used of a physically broken fishing net. In Mark 1:19 and Matthew 4:21, when Jesus called James and John into ministry with Him, they were in the process of "mending" their fishing nets. They were mending the holes in their net so the fish would not fall through. This restoration could easily involve a conflict between two people. Holes in their relationship need to be mended. This process involves healing relationships through forgiveness. These passages will be referred to as you read.

This book is a completely original work on reconciliation and forgiveness. It is not based on other books that I have read and simply collated. To produce this work, I carefully

3

read through the entire New Testament verse by verse and meticulously perused the Old Testament paying particular attention to the Psalms and Proverbs. As I read, categories were built from the individual passages, rather than a set of preconceived notions. These numerous categories became the individual biblical principles found in each chapter. Every passage was studied in its historical, grammatical, and scriptural contexts. Then, I compared my interpretations with those of past and present scholars. After this study, I have attempted to follow these biblical principles in my own personal life and also utilize them in my pastoral counseling practice. I have seen the Holy Spirit use them to transform relationships of all kinds.

One last thought. At the end of each chapter, I discuss a counseling experience. Due to confidentiality, none of these are based on one particular counseling situation. Instead, I have mixed together common elements I have seen, details from books and films, bits from my own life and the lives of people I have known, and thoughts from my imagination to create a situation where the biblical principles discussed in the chapters can fully be applied. These are composites of real-life situations. Read, learn, and apply. I commend you to the Lord and His Word (Acts 20:32).

Chapter 1

Involve God First

The first important step in the reconciliation process is the recognition that no matter who else we have sinned against; we have sinned against our God first. Therefore, when we have transgressed someone, we must initially ask God for forgiveness and reconcile with Him before we reconcile with others (see Introduction). It is His law that was broken.

A Typical Scenario

Have you ever had or heard a conversation with a spouse, parent, child, or friend that went something like this? You say or hear, "Oh, I will also tell you something else! (Person responds.) No, that is not the way it was! (Person responds again.) No, that is what you think it was, but it is not at all the way we had decided! (Person responds again.) No, I'm not going to do it that way! (Person responds again.) No, at the very beginning we did not decide to do it that way!"

Even as we are arguing, we know thirty minutes later the conviction of the Holy Spirit in us will come upon us. As we expected, the argument is over, and no one has won. We are sitting alone reviewing the conversation in our minds in a self-righteous state blaming the other person. Then the Holy Spirit begins His convicting work in our hearts. We think, "Okay, maybe we contributed to the argument." Then we stop ourselves and realize that we actually started the whole argument in the first place. Either way, we must return to the person we transgressed and work things out with them. This is God's will; yet this is not the first step.

A Scriptural Principle

Before we take the important step of reconciling with the person, we must first ask our God for forgiveness. The first principle in the forgiveness and reconciliation process is "we must recognize that our sin is first against God." Yes, we are arguing with our spouse, parent, friend, or neighbor, and we have violated that relationship but that's not the first issue. Our relationship with Almighty God, our relationship with our Master and Lord comes first and we have transgressed Him as we transgressed the other person.

A Biblical Explanation

As we are arguing with our spouse, parent, or friend, we are actually disrupting our relationship with God first. Why? It is His standards and laws that we are violating. Therefore, before we can go to our spouses we must deal with Him. This is found in Psalm 51. David has just committed the sins of adultery and murder which have been exposed. David opens the psalm crying out for God's mercy. He begs God for the forgiveness of these horrible transgressions and asks Him to wash him thoroughly from these sins and make him clean again. Then in Psalm 51:4, David utters, "Against you, and you only, have I sinned, and done that which is evil in your sight; that you may be proved right when you speak, and justified when you judge."

The word translated "only" in the English does not refer to God as the only one transgressed. Instead, it has the idea of "separate from." David is stating that His transgression against God was completely separate, wholly different, and stands alone when compared to anyone else that has been transgressed. He had sinned against Bathsheba, Uriah, their families, and even the nation of Israel as their leader, but this cannot be compared to the gravity and the seriousness of his sin against God. Why? God is above all else in the universe (Psalm 115:3). He is the ruler of all nations (Psalm 22:28) and the sovereign God (Ephesians 1:11). God is the law giver, and His law has been transgressed (James 2:10; 4:12). Most of all, His Son is our Lord (Romans 10:12-13). He was present listening to the conversation as we argued. He stands before us in every transgression. He must be asked for forgiveness.

The others transgressed do not set standards of behavior. God alone does. The Lord must be dealt with on a separate and utterly divine level before all others in the transgression. In Psalm 41:4, David again takes up the lament of his sins which brought reprisal from his enemies. The king cries, "I said, 'Yahweh, have mercy on me! Heal me, for I have sinned against you.'" Then this great king paints a beautiful picture of the relief he experiences in forgiveness. In Psalm 41:11-13, he shouts, "By this I know that you delight in me, because my enemy doesn't triumph over me. As for me, you uphold me in my integrity, and set me in your presence forever. Blessed be Yahweh, the God of Israel, from everlasting and to everlasting! Amen and amen."

In Psalm 79:9, the psalmist cries, "Help us, God of our salvation, for the glory of your name. Deliver us, and forgive our sins, for your name's sake." Here again is this requesting of forgiveness by God's children as expressed by the writer. This is critical in understanding the reconciliation process with others. We must reconcile with God first because He is the Supreme Being and His Son is Lord and Master of our lives. In Matthew 6, the disciples asked Jesus to frame a prayer for them to follow. In verse 12, Jesus uttered, "Forgive us our debts, as we also forgive our debtors." An essential part of our prayers is asking God the Father for forgiveness. What an amazing thing it is to be able to come before our loving God and ask for forgiveness! When we arrive at His throne in prayer as His children, we will find a God who is ready, willing, and able to forgive any transgression! No one understood this better than King David.

When we sin against God, He never forsakes us. Instead, God waits in readiness for our return to Him in repentance and confession. David acknowledges this in his Psalm 86:5, when the king wrote, "For you, Lord, are good, and ready to forgive; abundant in loving kindness to all those who call on you." This God of ours is ready to forgive when we sin. He is full of love and kindness to all who call upon Him. Then in verse 8, he shouts, "There is no one like you among the gods, Lord, nor any deeds like your deeds." In the midst of God's willingness to forgive, He only demands that we come to Him first to reconcile our relationships. He is our Lord; we must humble ourselves before Him in repentance, before we humble ourselves before others.

An Ancient Portrait

David was a mighty man of God, but he struggled with his passions. This led sometimes to terrible wickedness. His most infamous sin against God occurred in 2 Samuel 11-12. King David was the second ruler of Israel and a great King. In the days of good weather, Israel would go out to battle. In one such battle, David remained in Jerusalem. One evening the king was up on the roof of his palace relaxing (the roof was used in that part of the world much like a backyard patio is used in the western world). He noticed a beautiful woman bathing in the privacy of her home and wanted her.

David was king and could have any woman he wanted whenever he wanted her. So, he commanded his servants to bring her to him. He was the king, and she could not refuse. After he had his way with Bathsheba, David sent her home expecting absolutely no consequences. Sometime later, one of her messengers arrived and she told the foolish king that Bathsheba was pregnant. Now, what would David be able to do? Of course, he would try the first thing many people do when they are caught which is to cover it up. So, a clever idea came to him. He would call Uriah, her husband and a soldier, back from the battlefield. When he returned, Uriah would sleep with Bathsheba and think her child was his; the king directed his commander Joab to return Uriah to him.

After greeting David, Uriah was sent home. He felt that he could not return to his home and enjoy the fruits of his marriage while his fellow soldiers were in battle. Instead, he slept at the door of the king's house with the king's servants. When his majesty was informed that Uriah did not return home, he summoned the man and questioned him. Uriah responded by indicating that he could not possibly take any pleasures while the Holy Ark in Israel was under siege. He could not conceivably rest while his fellow soldiers were still in battle. It simply would not be respectable.

Now what was the king going to do? David conjured up another plan; he would invite Uriah to stay in his palace for the night and enjoy a magnificent meal with much drinking. Once her husband was fully intoxicated, the man would lose this silly notion and sleep with his wife as David had. The Scriptures indicate that King David made him drunk. This monarch probably insisted that Uriah continue to drink, even over the husband's protests. When Uriah finally left, David felt assured that his plan would work. Once again, the king underestimated this soldier of his. Even in his drunken state, Uriah refused to return to his home. He was not going to enjoy his wife and home when his fellow soldiers were in battle. Instead, he stayed with David's servants. At this point, David was done with his attempts to coerce this man to sleep with his own wife. The king commanded Uriah to resume his duties on the battlefield. The soldier was given a letter to personally hand to Joab, the commander of David's troops. In that letter was the King's final scheme and Uriah's death knell. Joab was to assign this obstinate soldier to the front lines of battle.

At an opportune time, the troops all around him would withdraw, and Uriah would be killed in battle. This will make it look like Uriah was a war hero, leave Bathsheba a widow, and allow David to take her as his wife. He would be able to raise his child without disgrace. Perfect! When the news came that Uriah had been killed, it was finally over. The problem had been solved. King David must have sighed in relief.

After the time Uriah's wife's mourning was completed, she became David's wife. All of this was done as if the Lord had not been around. All along the way, God must have been too busy with other things to even notice what he had done. Big problem! God Almighty had viewed the entire mess, and it was evil in His sight. When no one was looking, God was still there. When secret plans were being made and executed, God was present, and His laws were being broken.

Sometime later, Nathan, God's prophet, entered David's palace with a story to tell the great king. It was time to indict David for his foul play before the Lord. Nathan stood before David to seek his advice concerning a situation that he had encountered between two different men. Nathan described a city where two men lived, a rich man and a poor man. This rich man had much wealth, but the poor man had only one little ewe lamb. The poor man loved this lamb and treated it like his own child. When a traveler arrived and resided at the house of the rich man, a lavish meal had to be prepared and served. Rather than taking his own lamb, the rich man took the poor man's lamb, cooked it up, and served it.

King David did not even wait for the prophet to finish his story. He immediately declared that the rich man should be killed. Before he was to die, the man should make restitution fourfold for what he had done. Nathan stared directly at the king and declared that David was the rich man in his story. With this recognition of David's heinous sin came a series of judgments pronounced upon David from God Himself. How could David have done such a thing before God? It is easy he just pretended God was not there. Yet, He was. After this incident, King David repented of these sins and asked God for forgiveness. This is when he wrote Psalm 51.

He did not initially rush off to reconcile with Bathsheba, her family or Uriah's, or anyone else involved. First, he had to face His Lord God. When we sin against someone, we must recognize we have sinned against God and reconcile with Him. Once this occurs, we can concern ourselves with others. In fact, we will have the right heart and mind to be truly humble enough to reconcile with them.

A Modern Anecdote

Sometime ago, a married couple came into my counseling office to discuss a drinking problem his wife had. It came to a boiling point when the husband found his wife lying on the front lawn of his house in the morning. She was wearing her pajamas, and the lawn sprinklers were running. She was almost completely unconscious and not aware she was even getting wet. He helped her get up, and she stumbled into the house. Eventually, they got into a huge argument accusing one another of instigating the drunken behavior in the first place. As with many issues in relationships each contributed to the wife's constant drinking in different ways. It turns out that the husband was always annoyed at her for a variety of habits she had displayed during their marriage. As a result, he would pick at her and criticize her for many of the things she did. He did not like the way she left the dishes on the sink to dry or how she folded the towels. The house was not clean enough for his tastes and the list went on and on. Rather than argue and fight over the issues, the wife decided it would be much easier to drown the husband out. She did this by drinking.

The more he picked on her, the more she drank. The more she drank, the more he picked on her. Until finally all of it had gotten so out of control, their marriage was on the line. Divorce was eminent. When they were facing each other, they felt justified in their actions. After several sessions of discovering what was really happening, I stood them face to face before the Lord. He was their Savior and Master. What did Jesus think about their behavior (according to the Bible)? Once in front of the Lord, their inappropriate actions came to light. There are many ways to do things. Both partners had brought into their relationship a different approach to doing the dishes and laundry, cleaning the house, and washing the cars, just to name a few.

The Bible does not speak to many of the issues directly but does indicate that both partners must love, respect, and understand each other (Ephesians 5:33; 1 Peter 3:7). Neither partner was taking the time to do this by listening to the other. Instead, one argued, the other drank. Differences between people can never be resolved through yelling and drinking. The Scriptures are clear that believers are not to argue or quarrel (2 Timothy 2:24; Proverbs 18:19; 20:3; 22:10). Christians are never to be drunk (Ephesians 5:18; Romans 13:13; Psalm 69:12). This approach dishonored the Lord. This is not how Christ desires couples who are fellow heirs of the grace of life to behave toward each other (1 Peter 3:7). The Lord expects them to treat each other as He treats His own church (Ephesians 5:23,25,31).

After several sessions, each one could now see what their responsibility was in the relationship and how they had to behave. This required apologizing, accepting the repentance, and beginning again. Yet, the Lord could not be left out. He comes first. I sent them to the Father to reconcile with Him. Though they had hurt each other, they were hurting Him first. His laws had been broken, and they were not following His Word. Today, they are living with each other in a more mutually loving, understanding, and respectful way before the Lord.

The key to the resolution to this entire problem was to stand before God and answer to Him first. When we think we are only accountable to our spouses or others, then it is easy to continue the sinful behavior and not reconcile. When the Lord God, master of our lives, enters the conflict, then our minds can become clear, and the right response will come through the Holy Spirit.

Chapter 2

Leave Nothing Out

In the first chapter, we learned we must recognize that we are sinning against God first. Therefore, we should reconcile with Him before attempting to reconcile with the person we may have wronged in a relationship. As we walk into God's presence to ask for forgiveness, we must realize God knows the entire story and every detail of what we have done. As we confess our transgressions, we must admit to all of them holding nothing back.

A Typical Scenario

Have you ever had or heard a phone conversation with a customer representative that went something like this? You say or hear, "No! The item that you gave me is not working. First, I talked to you, and then you put me on hold, and sent me to somebody else. She also put me on hold and sent me to another person and he placed me on hold while I was talking. Then, I was disconnected. I had to call back! This is the third time I have called about this same exact problem. Obviously, none of you know what you are doing! (Person responds.) Okay! Fine! Goodbye!"

We all have had this kind of interaction with a customer service representative of a company. Then sometime later, we suddenly start feeling guilty for how poorly we treated the representative. Then we think, "Well, nobody saw it. Nobody is here. Nobody is around! So, what is the harm?" This couldn't be further from the truth. There is one person who sees everything that we do. He is the invisible observer of all our good and evil behavior, and nothing escapes His gaze. This person is God. We may attempt to conceal a small or minute detail of what we did to others we have hurt in a relationship, but we cannot hide it from our Father. We may think unkind thoughts about people, even say something evil to someone about them, or do something in secret that is against them, but God sees it all. When we ask Him for forgiveness, these should not be left out. Everything should be confessed as the Holy Spirit brings them to mind. This is essential in our relationship to the Lord.

A Scriptural Principle

The second principle is "we must know that God knows all our sins, so we must own up to all of them." Sometimes, when we go to ask for forgiveness from someone, we do not want to accept all of the responsibility we had in the sin. We want to leave out some of the words or actions which may embarrass us the most or lessen our responsibility. At other times, we like to alter the story slightly to make us look a little better; this is not the way God deals with things. God desires us to confess to Him everything we said or did, not just what we might feel is expedient, convenient, or even less embarrassing to us.

A Biblical Explanation

There may be times, where it would be too hurtful and not edifying to disclose everything, we thought or may have said in private to someone we have wronged, but we should confess these to God. As a result, when we confess our sins and ask for forgiveness to the ones we have wronged, none of the important details will be left out. We will take the true responsibility we had for what happened.

16

Confession before God involves the acknowledgement of all our sin. In Psalm 32:3-4, David describes the torment he felt when he refused to confess all his sins and kept them bottled up inside. He sobs, "When I kept silence, my bones wasted away through my groaning all day long. For day and night your hand was heavy on me. My strength was sapped in the heat of summer. Selah." Then in the next verse, he finally acknowledges all his sin. In Psalm 32:5, he continues, "I acknowledged my sin to you. I didn't hide my iniquity. I said, I will confess my transgressions to Yahweh, and you forgave the iniquity of my sin. Selah." Then King David describes the incredible relief and release he experiences. In Psalm 32:11, he adds, "Be glad in Yahweh, and rejoice, you righteous! Shout for joy, all you who are upright in heart!"

When Solomon cries out for the forgiveness of his people, it is for all their transgressions. In 1 Kings 8:50, he proclaims, "And forgive your people who have sinned against you, and all their transgressions in which they have transgressed against you; and give them compassion before those who carried them captive, that they may have compassion on them." We must admit every single detail of what happened between us and the person or persons we transgressed. God wants all confessed before Him.

In Psalm 90:8, Moses acknowledges this when he asserts, "You have set our iniquities before you, our secret sins in the light of your presence." Both Moses and the nation of Israel had a problem with sin, and he states that their iniquities and sin were before the Lord, even the hidden ones. These secret transgressions that no one knows are exposed in the light of God's presence. The light of God's holiness brings to light all our sins, even the ones hidden from all. Moses is explaining that the Lord sees all our sins. No iniquity can be hidden from Him. Once we are cognizant of His continual presence, His light exposes our sin.

Why do we often attempt to cover up the evil we do from God? He knows us completely. In Psalm 139:4, David cries aloud, "For there is not a word on my tongue, but behold, Yahweh, you know it altogether." Even before any word is spoken by us, it is already before His eyes. Nothing can be hidden; everything must be confessed (if we know about it). When we start the process of reconciliation, we all must first recognize that we have transgressed God's law and should confess everything to Him.

So, we must go before God with every thought, word, and action and lay them bare before Him. How do we do this? Through prayer, we ask the Holy Spirit to convict us of any transgression in the breakup of the relationship that we have committed. One of the responsibilities of the Holy Spirit in our lives is to convict us of sin (John 16:8). How does He do this? In Psalm 139:23-24, David beseeches, "Search me, God, and know my heart. Try me and know my thoughts." Then he adds, "See if there is any wicked way in me and lead me in the everlasting way." He entreats the Lord to show Him where he has failed. Can we imagine the power of asking the Lord to convict us of our responsibility in an incident in our relationship with a spouse, parent, friend, fellow student, teacher, or co-worker? Are we not always reviewing in our minds what they did, when we should really be reviewing what we did!

As we engage in this prayer, we should be searching the Scripture. Conviction comes from the Holy Spirit through the truth of the Word of God. In Hebrews 4:12, the author of Hebrews explains, "For the word of God is living and active, and sharper than any two-edged sword, piercing even to the dividing of soul and spirit, of both joints and marrow, and is able to discern the thoughts and intentions of the heart." The Scriptures can go deep into our hearts and discern thoughts, motives, and intentions. Then God will convict us of them.

In Psalm 119:175-176, this amazing psalm ends with, "Let my soul live, that I may praise you. Let your ordinances help me. I have gone astray like a lost sheep. Seek your servant, for I don't forget your commandments." When we have gone astray the commandments in His Word guide us back.

The best way to do this is to go step by step through every thought, word, and action in the transgression. We should judge each one according to the Word and depend on the Holy Spirit to guide us. Notice, we go through our actions, not the other person's. Often, when we recount a falling out between us and others, we carefully judge their thoughts (inferred by us), words, and actions; then, we get angrier and angrier, sometimes even letting ourselves off the hook in the light of their transgression. This is not God's way. We are responsible for our actions before God, not theirs.

An Ancient Portrait

In Genesis 1-3, we are given the story of Adam and Eve as they walked with the Lord God in the Garden of Eden and their subsequent fall from His grace. God created man and placed him in a garden. Adam was given the responsibility to name the animals and subdue the earth. God told Adam that He could eat of all trees of the garden, except for the Tree of the Knowledge of Good and Evil. As Adam named the animals, it became evident there was not a companion suitable for him as there was in the animal kingdom.

The Lord God saw that it was not good for Adam to be alone and proceeded to create a woman for him. God put Adam into a deep sleep and then took from his body one of his ribs and formed that into a companion for him. When Adam awoke, he declared that the woman was now bone of his bones and flesh of his flesh. She was taken out of him.

As a result, a man is to leave his father and mother and cleave to his wife. They will join together and become one flesh. This is when God created marriage. While Adam and Eve were in the garden and enjoying its many fruits and God's presence, suddenly a serpent appeared. We know that this was the Devil, but Eve did not know. The Serpent asked Eve about the Tree of the Knowledge of Good and Evil. When she said that it would essentially kill them if they ate of it, he disagreed. Instead, he told Eve that if she ate of it, her eyes would be opened, and she would be like God. Nice thought! Be Divine! Big Lie!

So, Eve looked at the tree. She saw that it was good for food; it delighted her eyes and would make her wise like God. She grabbed its fruit and ate. Then she handed it over to Adam and he ate it also. Suddenly, they realized that they were naked. Why? For the first time, they understood lust and evil desire, so they sought to cover themselves with leaves. They wanted to remove the shame they felt at being naked. Then they heard God coming. Now what were they going to do? Of course, they decided to hide from God.

They wanted to conceal their sin from God. So off to the bushes they went. Did they really think they could get away with this? Yes. Do we really think we can hide our sin from an all-knowing God? Yes, we really do. We fool ourselves by simply committing the sin without any thoughts of God. Put Him out of our mind while we fight, argue, yell, scream at someone and pick Him up later on. Perhaps, this is exactly what Adam and Eve also did. Where were their thoughts of God while they were being tempted?

Of course, God knows exactly where they are. God knows everything. He began making sounds as He approached, so the couple would know He was on His way. This was their first chance to admit to everything they had done. Instead, they hid themselves because the two were naked. They were more concerned about the situation of their nakedness, then the fact that they had just transgressed the Lord God. Are we not like that? We can get so wrapped up in the situation; we forget He is right there being transgressed.

Then the Lord God called to Adam and asked him where he was. Here God provided another opportunity for them to spring forth from their hiding place and admit all they had done. Instead, Adam explains that they had hid themselves because they were naked. God then inquired as to how they knew they were naked and whether they had eaten from the tree. Adam responded with man's first real excuse for his sin which will lead to a long history of excuses. He blamed the Lord and His wife. His wife blamed the Serpent.

There is a whole lot of finger-pointing at each other not at themselves. Adam blames the Lord God for giving him the woman in the first place. This action created the whole mess. The woman, Eve, blames the Serpent for his trickery. It was entirely someone else's fault; of course, they would think that as we do. Though not really mentioned directly, we know they admitted all of their sins, but the damage had already been done. The human race had fallen.

Believe me, we all have our excuses why the relationship was fouled up, and it is never our fault! We are the victims! Had our wives, husbands, sons, daughters, fathers, mothers, friends, acquaintances, co-workers, fellow students, or even customer service representatives acted any differently, we would not have reacted the way we did! Does this not sound familiar? We want to always be the victim! If we can blame someone else, we do not have to carry the full guilt for the destruction of the relationship. Unfortunately, that doesn't work for God, and it did not work for Adam and Eve. God desires people to take responsibility for their sins.

A Modern Anecdote

Many of my male clients have struggled with the evil of pornography. One such husband came to my office with his wife livid over his many mental affairs. While weeping, she recounted the evening she had found him in a compromised position lounging at his computer. As her emotions flooded out of her, he sat slumped over with his head down quietly muttering how difficult this all was and how embarrassed he felt. It was an utterly sad day for their relationship, but they desired to overcome this predicament with God's help. They wanted a strong marriage once again. Unfortunately, this problem can have multiple reasons for the issue to begin and multiple different reasons for the issue to have continued. It took some time to fully discover all of the factors involved and the extent to which the husband had actually sinned. Needless to say, pornography is a sin of the heart. It is sexual immorality of the heart (Matthew 5:28; 1 Corinthians 6:18; Galatians 5:19). There were many nights and more websites than he could even recall.

As I met with him individually, he was even too ashamed to disclose the full extent of what he had seen, nor could he admit everything he had done to his dear wife. Also, he could not even remember the many sites he had visited because the whole thing was a huge blur in his mind. A full disclosure to his wife was not necessary. This believer was accountable to His God first, and He would confess all of it to Him and Him alone. I did not need to know every detail to help him. His dear wife did not need to be traumatized by all that he had done. All of it was confined solely to his computer and the now permanently deleted images it bore.

Yet, to begin their healing process, this husband had to acknowledge that God had been there all along and he had done such evil in His presence. I will always remember that day he cried to the Lord in my office mumbling silently his sorrow while confessing the minute details of His sin to His Savior and Lord as I sat next to him praying. The man knew that Jesus Christ was forgiving him even as he was uttering quietly his many transgressions.

Then the healing process was initiated with his wife as he confessed to her his sins, and she forgave him. Over a course of time, these unrighteous practices were put away and fully replaced with holy ones that honored the Lord (Galatians 5:19-25; Ephesians 4:25-32). He battled with his flesh to keep from stumbling, and she battled with hers to fully forgive him. Eventually, victory came on both their parts, and the issue was finally settled in their relationship. I must mention one last thing. During the process, the man's wife realized that some things she did and did not do concerning their sexual interactions contributed to his problem. She realized that she had not fulfilled all of her responsibilities sexually to her husband. She took that before the Lord and to her husband.

Chapter 3

Admit Your Sin

When we have committed a transgression toward another person, we should reconcile our relationship with God first. When we approach God, we should leave nothing out. We are to take all of the sins we are responsible for in the breakdown of a relationship with someone to Him and admit our sin. This chapter explains the confession process toward God as outlined in Scripture. When this properly occurs, we will experience His full forgiveness and be ready to approach the other person we have transgressed.

A Typical Scenario

Have you ever been angry or upset because you received a traffic ticket that you perceived was unfair? Perhaps you described it to someone like this, "I am so angry and upset. The officer said I was reckless driving and gave me a ticket. Can you believe He said that I was eating a cheeseburger while I was driving? Well, you know what? I was. What's wrong that? A lot of people eat cheeseburgers while they're driving. Then, he said that I was texting, while I was eating the cheeseburger. Yeah, so what? I was texting, but I can still drive. You see, I can put my knees up on the wheel and drive that way. Oh, yes, he also wrote on the ticket that I had my dog on my lap which was distracting me. After I stopped texting, I used my electric shaver on my face. He must have been following me for a long time. How dare he give me a ticket? Doesn't he have anyone else to follow? There are a lot worse drivers out there than me. I certainly let that officer know how I felt about this ticket!"

Though the above is rather tongue-in-cheek rendering of a traffic ticket incident, it is meant to demonstrate how we often rationalize our mistakes, rather than admit them. We often try to figure out a way to get out of what we did that was wrong, instead of owning up to it and admitting that we had erred. This we must do!

A Scriptural Principle

The third principle in the reconciliation process is "we must fully repent of our sins and confess them before God." Often times, when we think of repentance, we may assume it simply means to be sorry for our sins. It actually has a fuller and broader meaning which encompasses three different aspects. True biblical repentance involves the admission of our sins, the sorrowing over those same transgressions, and the turning from those iniquities in a direction that is more righteous.

A Biblical Explanation

It is important to note that repentance does not end at the moment of salvation. True believers in Christ will constantly be recognizing the sins that they are committing and asking God for forgiveness. This is not just an eternal issue but a relational one. When we received Christ as Savior and Lord, all of our sins were forgiven from the past, present, and future (Colossians 2:13-14; Romans 8:1). In our relationship with the Lord upon this earth in the flesh, we still confess our transgression. This restores our relationship with God in a relational sense. Then, any barriers between us and God are eliminated. John speaks to this in his first letter. Some were saying in the church that they had matured to such a level that they no longer sinned. John, the apostle, counters with a scathing response. In 1 John 1:8, he emphatically states, "If we say that we have no sin, we deceive ourselves, and the truth is not in us." Then in verse 10, he declares, "If we say that we haven't sinned, we make him a liar, and his word is not in us."

Those who claimed that they had never sinned or no longer sinned were simply lying to themselves, others, and God. The truth of His Word was not in them because this truth convicts us of sin.

Then sandwiched between these two convicting passages is what believers do when they realize that they have sinned. In verse 9, John proclaims, "If we confess our sins, He is faithful and righteous to forgive us the sins, and to cleanse us from all unrighteousness." The verbs "confess" and "forgive" are in the present tense which indicates continual action in present time. Believers are continually confessing their sins, and the Lord is continually forgiving them. Asking God to forgive us is a lifelong practice.

This is so important. As we continually repent of our sins and experience God's constant forgiveness, then it becomes easier and easier to ask for the forgiveness of others we have transgressed. Also, it makes it much less difficult to accept the repentance of others as they transgress us. As saints, we must recognize our sinfulness, or we might be destined to become angry, bitter, and judgmental people.

There are three aspects to the full concept of "repentance" in the Scripture. These are presented in various places by different writers in the New Testament. Repentance involves admitting the sins we have committed, then sorrowing and mourning over their wickedness, and finally turning away from them toward righteousness. These three elements are crucial in our repentance process. These three are anticipated as the Spirit convicts us of our sin.

The first is the admission of sin. To fully repent, we must admit that we have sinned. This means that Christians are to acknowledge that the thoughts, words, and actions that they had taken were indeed sins. Notice 1 John 1:9 again, "If we confess our sins, He is faithful and righteous to forgive us the sins, and to cleanse us from all unrighteousness." John uses a critical word to explain his meaning. The Greek word translated "confess" literally means "to say the same thing." Confession is to say the same thing about a thought, word, or action that God says about them. They are sinful. They are against God's law.

The second aspect of repentance is to mourn over those sins. In the Beatitudes, the Lord Jesus speaks of the spiritual characteristics of His children. Though these qualities appear physical, they really refer to spiritual aspects of his kingdom people. In Matthew 5:3, Jesus declares, "Blessed are the poor in spirit, for theirs is the kingdom of God." There is no virtue in being poor. He was speaking of those poor in their spirit. The Greek word translated "poor" means "bankrupt" and refers to the acknowledgement that His people know they are spiritually bankrupt in sin. This is the first aspect, we just discussed.

The Lord continues in verse four, "Blessed are those who mourn, for they shall be comforted." This remark speaks of mourning over our bankrupt condition before God as one mourns over the dead. It refers to a deep sorrow over our sin and wickedness which is the second aspect. When someone receives the Lord, they admit their sin and mourn, grieve, and sorrow over it. As we live our Christians lives, we will be constantly convicted of our sins and are to admit them to the Lord.

The third aspect in repentance is the repentance of sins. Though this word is used with a fuller meaning in defining the entire concept, it also has a unique meaning of its own. The Greek word translated "repent" means "to turn around in the opposite direction or change one's mind or behavior." We must turn around from our confessed sins and move in the opposite direction. We must commit ourselves to living differently. Luke records Peter's denial of even knowing the Lord in Luke 22:62 and how the apostle wept in sorrow and remorse afterward. Later, Luke records in Acts numerous sermons that Peter preached in great boldness for Christ. Peter clearly demonstrated that he had fully turned in the opposite direction from that sin. Of course, the Holy Spirit will provide the strength needed in order to accomplish this supernatural feat (Acts 2:4; Romans 8:13). Now, consider the response of Judas. In Matthew 27:3-9, he would not repent nor humble himself before the Lord Jesus and remove the guilt and sorrow through salvation. Instead, he simply killed himself to alleviate them from his life. This is the sorrow unto death.

As we interlace the three principles we have studied in these initial chapters, we clearly see how we are to reconcile our relationship with the Lord, before we can reconcile with others. The response of all believers when they have sinned against another will be to turn toward God first and ask Him for forgiveness. This is accomplished through the admission of their wrongs, sorrow over their sin, and a turning toward righteousness while leaving no sin in the transgression out. This is how we are to reconcile with God, our Father.

An Ancient Portrait

This repentance process is distinctly seen in the story of Achan's sin in the book of Joshua, chapters 6-8. Joshua was the commander of the nation of Israel after Moses died. He brought God's people to the land of Canaan. He was told by God to wipe out the people in this wicked land. This was due to the horrible atrocities of the Canaanites. These people were so extremely wicked that even their possessions were unclean. No one was to take any plunder in the battles. Only gold and silver and a few other items were to be collected for the Lord's house. God was very serious about protecting the purity of His people and standing against their evil.

The first city to be defeated in their quest was Jericho. As most know, the walls came down through a miraculous feat of the Lord, and the city was taken. Now it was time to move on to a place called Ai. Having sent out spies, they realized this would require a small army to conquer them. So, their leader Joshua would only need 3000 men, not the normal 30,000. The army closed in on Ai with great expectations of a mighty victory.

Instead, the people of Ai ran them off killing 36 men and causing Israel to retreat in humiliating terror. Where was the power of the Lord God? What had happened? Something had gone terribly wrong. Joshua threw himself before the ark and begged the Lord to tell him what had happened. He was fearful that once the Canaanites heard of their miserable defeat, they would be run out of the country. The Lord told Joshua that one of his people had taken items from the city that was to be devoted solely to the Lord. The commander would have to find the violator and cleanse the nation from this atrocity. The Lord Himself would point him out, so all would know the seriousness of obeying the commandments of God Almighty, the God of Israel.

God told Joshua to bring the people before the Lord the next morning, and He would identify the transgressor. First, each tribe of the nation was brought before the Lord, and the Lord God singled out the tribe. Then He divided the tribe into smaller and smaller groups until He arrived at Achan and his family. So, this man Achan was required by Joshua to stand before God Almighty and give Him glory and honor by admitting the sinful action he had taken. This is so crucial to our understanding of how to reconcile with God.

The admission of our wrongdoing glorifies the Lord God by recognizing His sovereignty and power over all people. Then Achan admitted his transgression in detail. In Joshua 7:20, the author recorded, "Achan answered Joshua, and said, 'I have truly sinned against Yahweh, the God of Israel, and this is what I have done.'" Notice, Achan admits he has broken God's law and sinned against God first. Then Achan describes exactly how he had sinned in verse 21. He explains this, "When I saw among the plunder a beautiful Babylonian robe, two hundred shekels of silver, and a wedge of gold weighing fifty shekels, then I coveted them and took them. Behold, they are hidden in the ground in the middle of my tent, with the silver under it."

Notice what the man did not do. He did not demonstrate any mourning over what he had done or committed himself and his family to living righteously from then on. He did not fully reconcile with God. Also, he did not reconcile with the people of Israel or Joshua. They had lost thirty-six lives and experienced a major defeat. Instead, he admits what he did, shows them where the possessions are hidden, and accepts the punishment. It appears that there was no repentance, mourning, and turning toward righteousness.

All of us deserve physical death the very first time we sin and every time after that (Romans 3:26). Yet, God displays tremendous mercy on us all. At other times, the Lord God determines that He will not show His mercy and grace in withholding physical death to teach His people an important lesson. This was one of those times. The perpetrators of this atrocity against God's holiness were taken out and stoned to death. All their possessions, including the possessions they had taken, were burned with their bodies. Then a heap of rocks was put over it as a memorial in order to teach future generations the seriousness of obeying God and honoring His holiness.

When we sin against others, sometimes we rationalize our actions and will not admit what we did, mourn over it, and turn the other way. This is not how God deals with us. We must stop the rationalization and make things right with the Lord which honors and glorifies Him. Once our relationship with Him is fully reconciled, we will be ready to reconcile with those we have wronged. These steps are critical in the forgiveness process.

A Modern Anecdote

Sometime ago, a young man entered my counseling office with his parents because they thought he seemed depressed and sad. Since he was twenty-three (an adult), I had to bid the parents goodbye. This young man had been through a difficult time growing up after his parents divorced. He had to live rotating weeks with each parent which made him miserable. The mother periodically dated a series of men he did not like, and the father married what he characterized as a cold and harsh woman. Needless to say, he was not happy in either place. Whenever he spent time with his family, he was depressed and sad. Whenever he spent time with his friends, he was happy and funny. This was an important bit of information worth noting.

After some sessions, it became obvious that he had failed to launch. The mother was strong and demanding and the father had barely noticed him. His opinion about issues that affected him did not matter to either parent. He developed the attitude that he would just "go with the flow." Rather than asserting himself, he merely complied. This gave him a sense of imprisonment and a lack of control over anything. As a result, he became extremely dependent upon both his parents. As he continually acquiesced, the young man was unable to develop a real concept of himself and a hope for the future. He blamed his failure to launch on the fact that his mother needed him. How did he come up with this idea? As the men flowed in and out, he basically fulfilled the role of her husband (not sexually of course but emotionally).

She took him places and did things only adults would do. Though he did not desire to go to coffee after a movie and talk about it, he did love feeling and acting like an adult. Yet, when decisions had to be made concerning buying clothes, or music, his school and social life, she made them. He was acting like her mother's husband in some areas and like a younger child in other areas. The two eventually developed an unnatural dependence on each other.

First, the mother had lost her husband and replaced him with her son. This is fairly common, and usually the parent is not even cognizant of the issue. God's blueprint embedded within a person is for he or she to be married (Genesis 2:18) with the exception of being singularly devoted to the Lord which Paul calls a "gift" (1 Corinthians 7:7, 32-34). When a spouse leaves, the blueprint does not automatically shut off.

Instead, one must replace the spouse with the Lord, not a child or a "live-in mate" (Psalm 68:4-6). Second, the young man should follow God's blueprint "to leave and cleave" (Genesis 2:24) or live singularly devoted to Christ. The Lord never intended for children to be living with their parents beyond the childhood years (Proverbs 22:6; Ephesians 6:4). Third, the father was distant and unwilling to raise his son in the things of the Lord and prepare him for manhood. His wife was constantly exasperating and inciting his son until he finally gave in (Ephesians 6:4).

Once this was discovered, it became time to reconcile the relationships and launch this young man into adulthood. This begins with repentance before the Lord. His mother had to be gently confronted for her mistakes. She had "to cut the umbilical cord" with her son both as her servant-child and as her surrogate husband. His father and stepmother had to be lovingly confronted for not taking the responsibility for teaching the son how to become a man and for exasperating him to the point of subservience to their every wish. Both mom and dad had to take responsibility for their divorce and his resultant predicament.

The son had to be confronted concerning his response to everything that had happened. The son had not assumed any adult responsibilities and launched himself from the nest. Instead, he had taken great advantage of the situation by relying upon the mother to meet the needs that a wife should have met, or he should have taken care of himself as a single man (e.g. preparing food, laundry, earning a living, cleaning up after himself). All responded according to their own unique timeline (not all respond immediately).

They repented, admitted their sin, sorrowed over those transgressions, and then turned from them and moved in a more righteous direction. Next, they began the restoration process with each other which took some time. Eventually, the young man's sadness and depression left him and was replaced with a new vigor and enthusiasm for his future. Finally, the young man launched into single adulthood by getting his own place and living his own life. His launching began with the family admitting to the mistakes and sins each had done to contribute to the problem.

Chapter 4

Accept God's Forgiveness

When we have sinned against another, we should begin the reconciliation process by approaching God. A Christian's relationship with Him has been damaged, and God must be dealt with first. To restore the relationship with Him, we are to spread out our transgressions before Him and take full responsibility for them. We are to admit that they are wrong and ask Him for forgiveness. The next step is to accept God's forgiveness with a sense of blessing and gratefulness.

A Typical Scenario

Suppose you suddenly awoke in the middle of the night and felt the full weight and burden of all your transgressions against God. Every sin you had committed started parading through your mind, and you began to write them down. You were completely honest and left nothing out. Wouldn't you write and write and write and write until your hand was so sore you could no longer hold the pen? Of course, I would too. Here is an important truth: since we are Christians, our long list of sins, transgressions, and iniquities from small to great have been forgiven! All of them are completely gone. It is important that we accept this by faith.

A Scriptural Principle

The fourth principle is "we must believe by faith that all our sins are forgiven in Jesus Christ with a sense of blessing and thankfulness." The moment we repented and received

Jesus Christ, all our past, present, and future sins and the punishment involved were washed away. What do I mean by this? At the very moment that we placed our faith in Jesus Christ, the penalty for all our sins paid at the cross was appropriated to us directly. Eternal life became ours with full, complete, and total forgiveness. Since this is a spiritual process, there may not have been a great feeling of relief or a tremendous sense of forgiveness at this defining moment in our lives. Instead, we should claim this forgiveness by faith.

A Biblical Explanation

To fully accept this forgiveness in our lives graciously and thankfully, we should understand exactly what happened at the cross. When we speak of forgiveness, we are speaking of two kinds of forgiveness. One concerns what occurred when we received Christ as Savior and Lord. Here the penalty that was paid was appropriated to us, our sins were forgiven, and we were declared righteous before God (Romans 8:1). The second occurs in our earthly relationship and fellowship with God and occurs as we confess our sins and ask Him for forgiveness (1 John 1:9). When I sin against my wife with an unkind word or action, she often forgives me even as I am sinning. Yet, when I go to her and ask for forgiveness and she grants it again (in a sense), all the barriers between us are removed. The relationship is fully restored because we each did our part and took our responsibility. Then I feel a great sense of blessing and gratefulness for her continual love, mercy, and grace. When the reverse happens, she feels the same.

Paul describes what happened on the cross in Colossians 2. In verses 13-14, Paul explained it in these critical words, "You were dead in your trespasses and the uncircumcision of your flesh. He made you alive together with him, having forgiven us all our trespasses, wiping out the certificate of debt which was decrees against us; and he has taken it out of the way, nailing it to the cross" (DEJ). Christ has taken the certificate of debt consisting of decrees against us and has nailed them to the cross. What are these "decrees?" The decrees are the judgments against us for every transgression we ever committed, are committing, or will ever commit. It involves all past, present, and future sins.

Standing before a righteous and wrathful God, we would have been judged and punished for all eternity. How many decrees against us would we have with a lifetime of sinning? More than we could possibly count! Our iniquities were paid for by our Lord Jesus Christ in his death and nailed to His cross. In Hebrews 9:22, the author of Hebrews declares in the final part of the verse, "Apart from shedding of blood there is no remission." Through the shed blood of the Lord, these sins and decrees were nailed to the cross and wiped away.

After our confession, we claim this great truth by faith and accept His forgiveness. In Romans 4:8, Paul explains our blessed state when he testifies, "Blessed is the man whom the Lord will by no means charge with sin." There is the sense of blessing and gratefulness. God, our Father, will not charge us with our sin. We merely accept this.

In Hebrews 8:12, the author says, "For I will be merciful to their unrighteousness. I will remember their sins and lawless deeds no more." Here he quotes Jeremiah 31:34, where God is directly speaking. Then in Hebrews 10:17, the author repeats this again, "I will remember their sins and their iniquities no more." In verse 22, the holy writer compares our full forgiveness to washing with pure water, "Let's draw near with a true heart in fullness of faith, having our hearts sprinkled from an evil conscience, and having our body washed with pure water." As saints confess their sins, they can imagine pure water flowing over them washing their sins away. If this truth does not bring a sense of blessing and thankfulness, what will? Will this not prepare us to accept the Lord's forgiveness, and then to forgive ourselves, others, or humbly ask for forgiveness? The affirmative answer to this question demonstrates how powerful truths are.

To better do this, we must understand the abundant grace that was bestowed on us because the Lord will require us to bestow the same to ourselves and others. In Ephesians 1:7-8, Paul portrays what Jesus accomplished in these words, "In whom we have our redemption through his blood, the forgiveness of our trespasses, according to the riches of his grace, which he made to abound toward us in all wisdom and prudence." Notice what the apostle states concerning God's grace. The words "made to abound" is only one Greek word meaning "to exceed a fixed number of measure to be over, abundant, excelling beyond."

His grace overflowed exceedingly beyond anything that could be measured in order to forgive. Notice it is "according to the riches of His grace." Paul did not say "out of" but, "according to" the riches of His grace. This grace is infinite having no bounds, and this makes His forgiveness infinite and without bounds. The word "riches" is a Greek word meaning "riches, wealth." According to the abundant wealth of His grace came forgiveness. It came when we received Jesus Christ. Moment by moment as we confess our sins, He forgives and forgives and forgives again and again.

We desperately need His "wealth of grace" because we not only sin repeatedly but commit some horribly grievous sins against God, ourselves, and others. Yet, God forgives all of them. There is not one sin that a believer can commit that was not dealt with on the cross of Christ. When we repent and accept this forgiveness, a tremendous sense of blessing and thankfulness pours forth from our lives. In Psalm 103:1-2, the psalmist testifies, "Bless the Lord, O my soul, And all that is within me, bless His holy name. Bless the Lord, O my soul, And forget none of His benefits." This sense of blessing results from all of the benefits that God bestows on us as His people. In the first part of verse 3, he mentions forgiveness, "Who pardons all your iniquities."

In Psalm 28:7, David testifies of his thanksgiving, joy, and blessing, "Yahweh is my strength and my shield. My heart has trusted in him, and I am helped. Therefore, my heart greatly rejoices. With my song I will thank him." In verse 8, he adds, "Yahweh is their strength. He is a stronghold of salvation to his anointed." What an amazing and incredible sense of blessing and thanksgiving pouring forth in praise of God! Yet, the Lord does not want His children to stop there. God desires for us to take our experiences and allow them to produce a willingness on our part to forgive ourselves and others. Then, we humble ourselves to ask for forgiveness.

An Ancient Portrait

A great example of this sense of blessing and gratefulness is seen in Luke chapter seven. When Jesus was in Galilee, the Lord was invited into the house of a Pharisee named Simon. At times, Pharisees would persuade the Lord to give a talk in their homes to various dignitaries. Sometimes, He was invited for the purpose of trapping Him in something He said. Other times, they were serious about his ministry and message and wanted to learn from Him. While Jesus was at Simon's table, a woman who had the reputation among the Jews of being a "sinner" (most likely a prostitute), entered the house with a jar of expensive oil. I am sure to everyone's amazement she began to wet the feet of the Lord with her tears and wipe them with her hair.

After this, she kissed Christ's feet and anointed Him with her oil. One would think that Simon and the others would be filled with empathy and compassion as they saw this poor woman kneeling before Christ. Instead, these religious men of Israel were stunned that Jesus even allowed such a sinner to touch Him. "Why did He have anything to do with her?" they must have thought. The scoffers viewed the entire scene with disgust. They reasoned that if this Jesus was truly the prophet He claimed to be, He would know how wretched that woman was.

They did not realize that she was in the middle of an act of deep repentance crying out for ultimate forgiveness. Her tears were her repentance, her anointing was her recognition of His Deity, and His acceptance was His forgiveness. As she experienced His forgiveness, her tears then began to flow from her sense of acceptance, blessing, and thankfulness. To open up Simon and the others' minds to the significance of the moment, Jesus told him a story of a lender who had two people who owed him money. One of the two owed him five hundred denarii (500 day's wages) and the other five denarii (5 day's wages). The lender then forgave them both. One was forgiven a large amount and the other a smaller amount. Then Jesus asked Simon to pick the person who would love this lender more. Simon responded that it would be the one with the larger amount.

The implication was obvious. This woman, who was such a sinner, was showing a greater love for Jesus because Jesus had forgiven a greater amount of her sins than others. What a testimony of His forgiveness and her love demonstrated through repentance, acceptance, and gratefulness! Then the Lord Jesus turned the tables on Simon and compared his treatment of the Lord with her conduct toward Him. He was a self-proclaimed righteous man, and she was a proclaimed sinner. Christ told Simon that he did not wash the Lord's feet when He entered his home (a custom due to the wearing of sandals), but this woman washed them with her tears and wiped them dry with her hair. Simon did not kiss the Lord when He arrived (a common greeting at that time), but the woman continually kissed His feet. Simon did not anoint the head of the Lord with oil (a common custom to remove the smell of travel, like perfume), but she anointed His feet. The implication was clear. Here is a simple contrast between her humility and care for Christ and Simon's distaste of Jesus.

Then the Lord pronounced His forgiveness of the many sins of the woman. He acknowledged her great love for Him as Savior and Lord. Then Jesus declared exactly what had happened. He had given her the very gift she had desired all along which was forgiveness. Now Simon and his guests would clearly understand what they were viewing. Christ demonstrated through this story the love and forgiveness He has for us, and the sense of blessing and thankfulness we are to have for Him. She was welcomed, and we are welcomed. She repented and found forgiveness, and we repent and find the same forgiveness. She greatly sinned and found pardon, and we greatly sin and find the same pardon.

When we come before our Lord and Savior in repentance, sorrow, and confession, we will receive complete and total forgiveness every single time. We received it all on the cross eternally, now we receive it all relationally. We merely have to accept it all with blessing and thankfulness. Then out of that experience of full forgiveness, we must go to those who have transgressed us and demonstrate that same forgiveness toward them. To those we have transgressed, we must show the same repentance. We must display that same forgiveness toward ourselves. What a God of forgiveness we have! What grace and mercy we continually have displayed toward us as He constantly forgives our sins. Now, we must show that same grace and mercy to others by forgiving them also.

A Modern Anecdote

A young lady came into my office one day after spending weeks in rehab for a drug addiction. She told me that though she had learned some good things at the center, it had still left her empty inside. She was clean but empty. She told me that she did not know where to go from this point. The young woman went to her pastor who often refers clients to me, and she was referred. She told me that she needed God and had heard that I could help her find Him. Her story was a tragic one. She described herself, her mom, and her dad as the perfect little family living in a huge country home in the Midwest.

While her mom stayed home and took care of the house, her father was one of the managers of an equipment rental company. As a girl, she was good in school and won many achievement awards. She could not remember one time that her parents had argued or exchanged unkind words. From her perspective all was well and extremely comfortable in her world.

Then one day when she was about eleven, her dad came home and said he had lost his job. Her mom and dad went into their room and had a terrible argument which she had never seen before. She was petrified. The police came later that night and hand-cuffed her dad and took him away. When she asked mom what had happened, she explained that her father had stolen a huge amount of money from the company to pay back gambling debts. Her mom had never worked a day in her life and did not know what to do. After a year, her parents divorced, and her life felt like it was over. Since her father had mortgaged the house to pay attorney's fees, there was no equity left. As a result, they sold the house for a loss and had nothing left. They were going to have to live with her grandparents in a big city.

At twelve, her world shattered. She felt as if it had gone from a picture-perfect home to a dirty little house in a dirty suburb where the lawns were brown and the people were tough. The school was old and loud, and no one would talk to her. Then one day a druggy-type girl befriended her. This girl taught her how to fit in. She took her shopping for cooler clothes, showed her how to do her hair and make-up, and introduced her to drugs and older more mature boys. From that day forward, it was one party after another, while her mother worked long hours. In high school, she was almost always high on drugs. Her relationship with her mother deteriorated until one night she just stormed off and never returned. After two husbands divorced her and three of her children were removed by social services, she decided it was time to get cleaned up.

The woman was twenty-nine and empty. Now, she was sitting in my office asking for help. So, I shared the good news of Jesus Christ with her. Our Lord God was willing to accept her with open arms in spite of what she had done. He was willing to forgive all her sins and rebuild her life into the beautiful image of His Son. The Lord would give her a new identity, a new family of God, and help her go back and reconcile with all of those she had hurt and had hurt her. When she came for the next session, she explained that she could not believe that God would forgive her. She felt she was a total "screw-up" as she called it. I told her, "When you repent and receive Jesus Christ, you have to believe that God has forgiven you by faith with blessing and gratitude. You will make other mistakes as a Christian and will again have to accept this forgiveness by faith." We prayed and she received Jesus Christ as Savior and Lord. Then we began the process of rebuilding her life now in Jesus Christ.

Chapter 5

Forgive Yourself All

When we sin against another, before we go to them to ask for forgiveness, we must first approach God. We admit our sins and leave nothing out. We mourn over them and make a commitment to act in a more righteous way. With a sense of blessing and gratefulness, we accept God's forgiveness. After this, we must fully forgive ourselves. The Lord God may forgive us, but we do not always forgive ourselves. At times, when the memory of a sin rears its ugly head, we may experience all of the regret, shame, and humiliation again. Then we may beat ourselves up over and over again. This does not have to happen; we can overcome this in Christ. This is why He came to free us from sin's grip.

A Typical Scenario

Perhaps, you have had or even heard a conversation with a friend, parent, sibling, child, acquaintance, co-worker, or fellow student which went something like this, when they asked you how you were doing? You say or hear, "I am fine. I am just fine. Everything is going great. (Pause.) No, really, I am doing great. Yes, that was a big mistake, humiliating and embarrassing, but I am okay with it. (A moment of silence occurs). No, what am I saying, everything is not fine. I am miserable and depressed. I will never get over what I did. I hate myself. The embarrassment was horrible. I cannot bear it! Whatever I do reminds me of how rotten I am!

A conversation like this describes how we may feel when we commit a terrible sin against someone. There lies a heavy weight of humiliation and shame upon us. Even after the sin has been confessed, the memory keeps returning whenever we see or hear something similar, in a book, movie, song, or experience we have. This may go on for days, weeks, or even years. Christians do not have to live with this weary load and strain. God desires for us to experience full forgiveness which includes the full forgiving of ourselves for the sin.

A Scriptural Principle

The fifth critical principle in healing relationships is "we must forgive ourselves for our sin as God has forgiven us." Once we have accepted God's forgiveness, we must turn our attention toward ourselves, before we turn it toward others. It is very difficult to restore a relationship with someone else, when we are still dealing with the sin within ourselves. This will make us feel defeated, broken, and unable to build the relationship anew. We do not have to carry this burden; instead, we can be free of it once and for all. We can be fully released from these self-imposed chains. Notice, I said, "self-imposed!" This kind of bondage comes from within. It needs to be identified and then dealt with.

A Biblical Explanation

To unchain ourselves from the bonds of our own lack of forgiveness, we must understand the source of the shame, guilt, and humiliation. This does not originate from the Lord. Once we confess the sins and accept our forgiveness by faith, it should all flow away. If it does not, then the flesh is the culprit. In Romans 7:20, Paul calls our sinful flesh the "sin which dwells in me." The sin principle resides in our physical bodies. The flesh (common word for this principle) desires to wallow in its own sin. It can be prideful, arrogant, and boastful, but it can also be insecure, worried, and unable to trust God. In our case, it is the voice inside us that says, "You are no good, pathetic, and just plain stupid! You will never overcome this moronic act. You fool! You idiot!" It chastises us like a vicious parent. It whips saints with the memories of their own mistakes over and over again.

The flesh has two powerful accomplices in its endeavor to lie to us: the world (1 John 2:15) and the Devil (John 8:44). The world or society of unbelievers enjoys watching God's people fall from grace and then scoffing at them (Psalm 1:1). This battle to overcome the guilt, shame, and humiliation of past actions pouring forth into full self-forgiveness can be fought using several biblical strategies. The first involves our minds. In our minds, we must "take every thought captive to Christ." In 2 Corinthians, Paul, the apostle, discussed the many false beliefs the saints possessed about him and their faith. Then in chapter 10, verse 5, he described his ultimate objective in all of his preaching and letter writing. He was "throwing down imaginations and every high thing that is exalted against the knowledge of God and bringing every thought into captivity to the obedience of Christ."

This is a simple concept when examined carefully. Every single idea or thought should be examined. Those thoughts that are contrary to the Scriptures should be discarded and those consistent should be embraced. In Romans 12, Paul explains how Christians can resist conforming themselves to the world, and it involves their minds. In verse 2, Paul states this, "Don't be conformed to this world, but be transformed by the renewing of your mind." Our mind is renewed in God's Word by discarding worldly thoughts and embracing God's thoughts. This then transforms us into His image. The saints forgive themselves and carry no guilt. They discard thoughts that condemn and embrace thoughts that forgive. How can this be practiced in our lives? We should speak to ourselves and identify the source of the negative thoughts. Then, we should replace them with new ones. I will often speak to myself and say, "I know these thoughts are from my flesh. God has forgiven me according to 1 John 1:9. I will not believe that God will hold this against me."

The second way to overcome our own lack of forgiveness is guard our hearts and minds in Christ Jesus. Paul exhorts the Christians in Philippians 4:6-7 to never be anxious about anything. Instead, we are to bring everything to our God in prayer with thanksgiving. That "everything" includes the sense of disappointment and guilt over a sin against a loved one. He then promises the peace of God which will guard our hearts and thoughts in Christ Jesus. The next two verses are often left out of a discussion concerning the removal of anxiety but are equally important. After we pray and turn these requests to God, we must think and act differently.

In Philippians 4:8, Paul adds, "Finally, brothers, whatever things are true, whatever things are honorable, whatever things are just, whatever things are pure, whatever things are lovely, whatever things are of good report; if there is any virtue, and if there is any praise, think about these things." Then in verse 9, he concludes with a general statement, "The things which you learned, received, heard, and saw in me: do these things, and the God of peace will be with you." Once we turn our requests over to God, we must change our thinking and doing. Our minds must dwell on honorable, just, pure, lovely, virtuous, reputable, praise-worthy things, while we behave in a way that is consistent with Paul and the apostles (righteous ways). The result will be peace in our hearts and souls. This will surpass any comprehension.

The third way to unchain ourselves from the bonds of our own lack of forgiveness is to deal with the memories of our sin. The memory system that God has imbedded in us was to learn from our mistakes. We put our hand in a fire and get burned. Through that experience, we create a memory. This helps us learn not to do this again. When we see a fire again the memory of our being burned returns and we are warned. This will work the same way with our sins. When we sin, we receive the consequences of our sin which includes shame, guilt, and humiliation before repentance. When we travel through life, many different triggers bring up those painful memories. We will need to rehearse within ourselves what we learned from the experience and then commit ourselves to never do it again.

These are basically reminders to be careful. They do not have to debilitate us. They will bring up some of the feelings we experienced when the problem occurred. This is what memory is supposed to do be doing, so we will not forget how "burned" we got. I usually say to myself, "I am glad I went through that experience. I will never do that again because the guilt, shame, and humiliation were so great." I will thank the Lord for His forgiveness and rejoice in Him. These strategies will help the saints let go of this difficulty.

An Ancient Portrait

A great illustration of this supernatural ability to forgive oneself is Peter (Matthew 26; Mark 14; Luke 22; John 18). In the Garden of Gethsemane, Jesus told His disciples that He was about to be betrayed, and all of them would fall away. Peter declared that he would never fall away. Jesus looked at Peter and told him directly that this very night before the cock crowed, Peter would deny Him three times. The apostle declared that he would die before he ever denied the Lord. Aren't we exactly the same way? At first, we think that we could never do some of the sins that others have done. Later, we find we have done the very same or similar thing.

This chief of the apostles could not even conceive of the fact that he would ever deny the Lord. Then the mob came. The leaders of the Jews dragged Jesus away. Peter followed Him to the courtyard of Annas, the former high priest. After he entered, a slave girl walked up to him and asked if he were one of the disciples of Jesus. Without hesitation, he denied that he even knew Jesus. Then Peter walked over and began to warm his hands in front of the fire. He was joined by some of the servants and officials. Again, he was asked if he knew Jesus. Again, Peter denied knowing Him. Finally, a servant of one of the officials noticed his accent. The servant proclaimed that not only did Peter have a Galilean accent, but he had actually seen him with Jesus. Peter responded by cursing, swearing, and proclaiming loudly that he did not know the man. Peter had the accent and was seen with Jesus by an eyewitness, but He still lied.

After this, Peter was so distraught that he went out and wept bitterly. He was genuinely repentant and sorrowful for this wicked deed. I am sure he confessed it to God. When he was restored by Jesus in John 21:15, it is never brought up again. It is never mentioned in his letters or in the book of Acts. Peter was a joy-filled, peace-filled, and thankful saint. He had accepted by faith his forgiveness and did not beat himself up over and over or churn it over and over in his mind. Peter found joy after their confessions, and we can find the same. This does not mean there were absolutely no consequences to Peter's denial. It is written in all four gospels as a testimony to what Peter did. The greater testimony was the courage and boldness Peter displayed after his fall. He went on to achieve great things for God.

Peter never dwelt on his colossal failure, nor did he forget it because he never denied the Lord again. In fact, on many occasions he stood boldly for the Lord Jesus. In his letters, he spoke of the courage of the other men of faith to encourage his brothers and sisters to remain strong. He also remained in truth and practiced righteousness himself while trusting God that he too was fully forgiven. Once we are able to fully forgive ourselves, we can forgive those who transgressed us or to ask for forgiveness of those that we transgressed.

A Modern Anecdote

In the world today, adultery has become a fairly common occurrence. This is a difficult situation for all involved. Some Christians think that adultery should always lead to divorce, but this simply is not the case. I have seen the Holy Spirit rebuild many marriages in which adultery occurred. A while ago, a married couple entered my counseling office in the pit of this debilitating situation. The wife was weeping, and the husband was completely distraught. He had been involved in a six-month long affair, yet they both wanted to save the relationship. As I was speaking to the husband, he began to shed tears and muttered, "Dr. Jones, I became that guy!" I asked him to explain what he meant by that comment. He told me that he was now "that guy everyone in his church, job, neighborhood, and community stares at, talks about, and avoids." Unfortunately, this situation could and does actually occur, but it is a transgression that can be forgiven (1 John 1:7; Colossians 2:13).

The husband was a very high-ranking city official. Often, his office would take in a group of interns and provide the experience they needed to complete their university training. He usually wasn't involved directly with the interns, but the one in charge was in the hospital preparing for surgery. One particular female intern did catch his eye, but he reminded himself how happy he was in his marriage. Also, he knew the Lord was watching. She traveled with him from time to time as he continued his work in the city.

51

Every single time she returned to his office, the woman was dressed more provocatively. Feelings were beginning to develop on both their sides, until finally she suggested they stay a little longer at his office to finish the city project that they were working on together. They could order in dinner. He knew that everyone had gone home for the evening but gave into the temptation. This critical working dinner turned into a powerful romantic encounter leading to a six month affair. He told me that all along he had mixed feelings about what he was doing but continued with the affair anyway. The woman was unsaved, unmarried, and was not at all bothered by it.

Finally, the wife found a receipt from a hotel in his wallet and confronted him. The husband confessed everything, and the wife demanded that he leave. He said good-bye to his four shocked children and went to stay with a friend. After some time, she realized how much she loved him and asked him to return home. He already had ended the relationship with the other woman. Over the weeks, many issues came to light from his childhood including how he was raised and the difficulties his father had with the same issue, his habits surrounding his purity, their lack of intimacy, and his lack of adequate safeguards. Many people think, "Oh, I can trust my husband or wife." The issue is not trust, it is a healthy fear of the flesh, the world (society and their values), and the Devil, and the devastation one can experience when these enemies of our righteousness are left unguarded and unchecked.

After dealing with each and every one of these factors, the process of forgiveness and reconciliation had to begin. The obstacle that caused the largest problem was not the wife and his children forgiving him, it was his unwillingness to forgive himself. He was filled with anxiety because he felt like he was wearing a large sign that read "Adulterer!" which everyone could see. He began to think every conversation was about him, and every look was a look of condemnation. Even this he could handle as part of the consequences of what he had done, but his inner voice kept condemning him.

The inner voice that haunted him was not his new man but his old man: the flesh. To relieve him of this constant condemnation, I shared with him key biblical concepts in this chapter. This provided for him the truth that the Spirit utilized to remove the mental sign and to allow him to fully forgive himself. The final and most critical step for their marriage involved the placing of various safeguards into his life which would rebuild the trust of his wife and children and prevent this sin from occurring again. Often this step is left out, but the setting up of safeguards (Philippians 3:1) to preserve his purity and the sanctity of their marriage bed (Hebrews 13:4) is crucial in rebuilding the relationship. This will also aid in the forgiveness process of his wife and his children as they literally watch him demonstrate over and over his commitment to his purity before God and them.

Chapter 6

Ask Others Next

When we have sinned against others, one of the most difficult things to do is to ask for forgiveness. Perhaps, we are too proud to humble ourselves. Maybe, we are fearful of their response. We could even be simply too ashamed to face them. This is a step that is often ignored, and we may even pretend the sin never happened. We simply go about our business as if everything is fine when it is not. Herein lies the problem: if we cannot do this with God, our Father, then we cannot do this with others. The Scriptures do not allow it. Whether the other person requests it or not, the Lord does.

A Typical Scenario

Have you ever had or perhaps heard a conversation like this concerning a father and his teenage daughter? He says, "I am not going to ask for forgiveness. (Wife responds.) Yes, I know I accused her and punished her for the dent in the car. (Wife responds.) I know now that the neighbor did it and not her, but I do not like her attitude. (Wife responds.) No! I will not ask her for forgiveness. Period!" Even though this typical father was wrong, he does not want to admit it. He refuses to ask his daughter for forgiveness. Have you ever felt that way about someone you know or love? Have you refused to ask for forgiveness from someone you have wronged?

The answer is obvious, we all have experienced this. Since he is a Christian, we know it will not be long before the Holy Spirit convicts him, and he will reconcile with his daughter.

If he does not, this will create a wall in their relationship. As he does this over and over again, this wall will grow taller and taller. Eventually, there will no longer be a relationship. All our relationships can fall victim to our unwillingness to ask for forgiveness and to reconcile. In the introduction to this book, I referred to three important passages indicating that God has only one way to restore relationships, and it is through forgiveness (Matthew 5:23-24; 18:15; Galatians 6:1).

A Scriptural Principle

The sixth principle is both obvious and natural. It is "we must reconcile our relationship with those we have sinned against by asking for forgiveness." This next important step simply involves asking for and then receiving forgiveness. This will occur first with God, then with the others involved. This was described in 1 John 1:9, "If we confess our sins, he is faithful and righteous to forgive us the sins, and to cleanse us from all unrighteousness with God." These Greek verbs are in the present tense which indicates continuous action in present time. In our relationship to the Father through Jesus Christ, we are continually confessing our sins, and the Lord God is continually forgiving our sins. This describes the life of a believer with God: confessing and forgiving. This does not describe the full forgiveness on the cross (Romans 8:1); instead, it explains relational forgiveness people bestow on each other as they fellowship together.

A Biblical Explanation

As Christians, we are constantly confessing, and God is constantly forgiving. It is the same way in our relationships with others. We are to behave in our relationship with others as we do with God: confessing and forgiving. In Luke 17:3-4,

56

this is exactly what Jesus affirms when He says, "Be careful. If your brother sins against you, rebuke him. If he repents [confesses and asks for forgiveness], forgive him. If he sins against you seven times in the day, and seven times returns, saying, 'I repent,' you shall forgive him." This confessing is the admitting of what we specifically did wrong. Then there is a mourning and sorrow over the sin. This leads to the final stage which involves turning in the opposite direction from what we did. We do this with God, and then we do the same with others.

This asking for forgiveness of those we have wronged is so obvious and is such a normal part of life. It is woven into our very fabric as human beings. When we are transgressed, we expect the person to come to us and ask for forgiveness. In Romans 2, Paul is discussing the conscience, and its place in the judgment of man. He explains that within people is a law God puts within their hearts, and they will be judged according to that law. In verse 15, Paul describes it, "In that they show the work of the law written in their hearts, their conscience testifying with them, and their thoughts among themselves accusing or else excusing them." When we hurt, or harm a person, we will have a natural desire to ask for forgiveness because it is written on our hearts.

Asking for forgiveness is one of those very natural things inside us. It is a law or rule within our nature. When we wrong people, we know innately that we must ask them for forgiveness. When people wrong us, we expect them to ask for forgiveness. This is so obvious to people that no one has to really teach them or explain to them that it must be done. This concept of "sinning against" someone can be found in several places in the Bible. One example is found in the life of Abraham. While living in the land of Gerar, he was afraid that the king would be attracted to his wife and kill him to take her for himself. So, Abraham asked Sarah to tell the king that he was her brother which she did. When the king took Sarah, as Abraham had predicted, his life was spared. Then God stepped in and stopped the king before he could violate her.

The Lord God told the king the truth about Abraham and closed the wombs of Abimelech's wife and female servants until he rectified the situation. In Genesis 20:9, Moses writes, "Then Abimelech [the king] called Abraham, and said to him, 'What have you done to us? How have I sinned against you, that you have brought on me and on my kingdom a great sin? You have done deeds to me that ought not to be done!'" Abimelech questioned Abraham as to how the king had "sinned against" him. Notice, this concept of "sinning against" others was a truth that was natural to all people.

This companion concept of "asking for forgiveness" once someone is sinned against is also found in Scripture. After Pharaoh had refused to listen to Moses and let God's people go, the land was overtaken by swarms of locusts. Pharaoh responded immediately by repenting of his rash actions. In Exodus 10:16-17, Moses described it in these words, "Then Pharaoh called for Moses and Aaron in haste, and he said, 'I have sinned against Yahweh your God, and against you. Now therefore please forgive my sin again, and pray to Yahweh your God, that he may also take away from me this death.'" Here is a clear example of what this "asking for forgiveness" looks like, though it is from such a hard-hearted man. Pharaoh admits his transgression against God first and then Moses.

In 1 Samuel 25, David encounters a foolish man named Nabal who refused to be hospitable toward David and his men while they were on a journey. David had been careful to make sure his men had treated Nabal's men properly and then asked for some provisions for their travels. This was an important cultural practice, since there were very few inns and places to eat on the road. Nabal, though very wealthy, refused to even acknowledge David. This was an offensive act on Nabal's part, and David was extremely offended. He immediately commanded his men to take up their swords to defend their honor.

When Nabal's wife, Abigail, discovered this humiliation of David, she quickly took action to protect her husband. She went out to meet David and took full responsibility for her husband's actions. She pleaded for forgiveness for the both of them. In 1 Samuel 25:23-24, the author describes their encounter, "When Abigail saw David, she hurried and got off of her donkey, and fell before David on her face, and bowed herself to the ground. She fell at his feet, and said, 'On me, my lord, on me be the blame! Please let your servant speak in your ears. Hear the words of your servant.'" Abigail admitted the transgression and displayed her sorrow over the whole incident. Then she provided David with all the rations that they needed for their journey. What gifts! This demonstrated her repentance as she turned in the opposite direction from what had been done. Ultimately, God judged foolish Nabal by taking his life, and this righteous woman became David's wife.

Paul himself alludes to this practice when he rebukes the Corinthians for accusing him of preaching to them in order to ascertain money. It was exactly the opposite. He was so concerned that they might think this that he worked in his tent-making trade and used the funds from other churches to support himself. Then he shared the gospel with them. In 2 Corinthians 12:13, he sarcastically questions, "For what is there in which you were made inferior to the rest of the assemblies, unless it is that I myself was not a burden to you? Forgive me this wrong." He requests them to forgive him for a wrong, which he did not do, but they had thought he had done. Though he is using sarcasm to make his point, we have a simple example of this principle of "asking for forgiveness" when someone has been wronged by us.

At times, people are afraid to ask for forgiveness because they might not receive a kind and gracious reaction from the person they transgressed. This does not matter. The reaction he or she has is entirely up to the Lord God. It only matters that we accept the responsibility for the sins we committed. Be forewarned, it may take some time to prepare ourselves fully for the confessing and repenting, and it may take time for the person we have wronged to forgive. That's fine! This is one of the many reasons the Christian life is called a walk because it involves one step at a time (Galatians 5:16). Why? The sin principle within all believers is strong and influential (Romans 7:14). If we are the ones who have sinned against another, we may prefer to pretend it never happened and move on. So, we may have to spend time in the Word and prayer to ask for forgiveness.

An Ancient Portrait

This process is so aptly demonstrated in the life of Joseph. His brothers were reluctant to ask for forgiveness when they sinned against Joseph. This story is found in Genesis 37-50. Most know the story of Joseph but are unfamiliar with their difficulty in asking for forgiveness. Joseph was hated by his brothers because he was the favored son. Also, he had two dreams that indicated his brothers would bow down, honor, and serve him one day. This enraged them so they sold him into slavery. Joseph was purchased by Potiphar, the captain of Pharaoh's bodyguard. During this time, he was put in charge of all that this man had. Yet, his wife yearned for Joseph. When he denied her advances, she accused him of attempted rape, and he was thrown into prison.

There, Joseph interpreted the dreams of two Egyptians. One was restored to Pharaoh's court and informed him of Joseph's interpretive gifts when the emperor wanted two dreams interpreted. The Pharaoh explained the dreams to Joseph and begged him for the interpretations from his God. This favored son of Jacob predicted that there would be seven years of plenty and seven years of famine in the land. He recommended that Pharaoh assign someone to gather grain into storehouses during the time of plenty and then distribute it during the time of famine. Pharaoh took his advice and appointed him over the entire kingdom at the age of thirty.

Several years later, his father Jacob began to experience the famine back in the land of Canaan. Jacob sent his sons to Pharaoh's court to buy grain. All went except Benjamin who was Joseph's blood brother. When his brothers arrived to purchase grain from Joseph, they did not recognize him. Yet, Joseph realized that he was in the presence of his brothers. He had to excuse himself to weep in private. Though Moses does not explain the tears, they appeared to be tears of joy. Though they had sold him into slavery, Joseph knew God's higher purpose for allowing it to happen. He had already forgiven his brothers for what they had done; even though, they had not asked for forgiveness. Isn't this what God does continually in our lives, since the entire debt of our sins were nailed to the cross (Colossians 2:14)?

Through a series of schemes, Joseph forced his brothers to bring Benjamin and eventually their father Jacob to Egypt. Finally, he revealed himself. After this, Jacob was brought to Egypt. His family was given a choice piece of land, and life in Egypt began. After a long period of time, Jacob eventually died. Now the brothers became fearful because they had not reconciled with Joseph. They had never acknowledged their evil before him, nor had they asked him for forgiveness. In

Genesis 50:15, Moses describes it in this way, "When Joseph's brothers saw that their father was dead, they said, 'It may be that Joseph will hate us, and will fully pay us back for all of the evil which we did to him.'" They were scared of Joseph and his great power, though he had shown nothing but love to them. In verse 16 and the first part of 17, they claim that their father Jacob had wanted them to tell Joseph to forgive them. We do not know whether Jacob had actually said this, but it seems obvious that they were fearful that their brother was going to put them to death.

Then the brothers finally did what they should have done from the beginning - ask for forgiveness. Moses continues, "'Now please forgive the disobedience of your brothers, and their sin, because they did evil to you. Now, please forgive the disobedience of the servants of the God of your father." Here they bring God into the picture and beg for forgiveness which is what He would want them to do. After this, they both wept in each other's presence, Joseph granted them his forgiveness and explained the Lord's purpose in it all. Joseph had to experience all of this to bring him to a position that he could save the entire nation of Israel who was not yet born but still in his loins and those of his brother's. He also could deliver others on earth who came to buy grain from Egypt. We don't know if Jacob had actually requested Joseph to forgive them or whether they lied to appease Joseph's anger. However, we do know that they did ask for forgiveness and humble themselves in confession, repentance, and sorrow before their brother Joseph.

Sometimes, the confession and repentance of people can be less than perfect but real and genuine. Again, we are all battling the flesh. Notice, they sent a message. There are times we have difficulty asking for forgiveness face to face. This is perfectly fine. A card, a letter, or even a text asking for forgiveness is very appropriate. Remember, much of the

New Testament was written as letters. What could be better confirmation of the appropriateness of writing letters than this? Though I would like to give a caution, some people we have wronged may desire a face-to-face reconciliation. This should be granted, if possible. What a great illustration of our principle of asking someone for forgiveness. So, if we have a broken relationship with our spouse, partner, parent, child, friend, neighbor, co-worker, fellow student, or even an acquaintance, then we must go to them, ask for forgiveness, and reconcile. This is God's only process for restoration.

A Modern Anecdote

Sometime ago, a man entered my office in an angry rage. He wanted equal custody of his children, but his ex-wife had moved them to another city. This would not allow them to share custody on a rotating weekly basis. I inquired as to the salvation of both him and his ex-wife. He indicated that they were both saved but not living the Christian life the way they knew God had wanted. They divorced, and both found someone else and just as quickly married. There were four children involved of various ages, and they were having a myriad of problems with them at home and in school. He wanted more access to them so he could be the father they needed, and the ex-wife was angry at him over the marriage and didn't want to give him any more time.

After several sessions, it was obvious to all of us that they had no biblical reason to end the marriage. They realized that they divorced over insignificant issues which had never been resolved. They let these simply built up over time until they claimed they were no longer "in love." This led to all the other problems including the custody issues. Since they were already married to someone else, they could not reconcile the relationship. Yet, they still had a relationship as mother and father. Their children needed a stable environment in both homes. This stability must come by aligning their new lives as close to the Lord's biblical blueprint for the family as possible. I asked each individually if they thought the other ex-spouse was a good parent. Each agreed.

As a result, the first aspect of their lives which must align more fully with the Scriptures was the children's access to both parents. Numerous times in the book of Proverbs and elsewhere, the inspired writers mention the teaching and training of both mother and father (Proverbs 1:8; 4:3; 6:20; 10:1; 15:20; 23:25; 30:17). So, the custody was legally changed to rotating weeks. Since discipline is the critical issue in the lives of children, they should together establish four or five general rules with similar consequences for both homes. We worked on other parts of this new custody agreement and living plan that would stabilize both environments for these children. Children do not stop being children, when parent's divorce. They must still be trained and disciplined.

The next step in the process would require the greatest power from the Holy Spirit. They must reconcile with each other and the children. This could only be accomplished by each of them asking for forgiveness of the other and then the children. Both of them had sinned in the marriage, both had agreed to the divorce, and both had disrupted the lives of all their children by being unwilling to follow God's biblical blueprint. They must let the children know that the way they are living was not God's blueprint, but through His grace and His mercy He would work in spite of it. This way they would not add this broken model to their own repertoire of the many actions they could take when they had difficulties in their marriages. This healing process would also lessen the children's own wounds from the divorce as they entered their adolescent and adult lives. These wounds cannot be ignored and are best dealt with early.

After asking forgiveness of each other, each parent sat in my office with each individual child. The father went first and then the mother. It was a beautiful and supernatural experience for all involved. Both parents sat before their children, humbled themselves, and asked for forgiveness from each one individually. Each one lovingly responded in their own way, "Yes, Daddy, I forgive you" and "Yes, Mommy, I forgive you." Then each was asked if they had something to confess to the parents concerning the wrong responses they may have made at home or in school in response to their parent's divorce (according to their age and understanding).

Each admitted that they were misbehaving and asked them for forgiveness and made a commitment "to be better." As each one spoke, I was praying and prompting them as necessary. Then we met together with the children and the new stepparents and explained the new stable living plan they would have. The joy on their faces was so rewarding. They looked at both parents and thanked them for trying so hard to make things right again for them. Children are much more aware and understanding than we might think they are. These new families had finally been reconciled through God's forgiveness.

Chapter 7

Humbly Make Restitution

Once we have asked for and accepted the full forgiveness from God for the sins we committed against another person, we must then go to them and ask for forgiveness. After this, we should offer them restitution, if needed. Though it is quite intuitive, often it is neglected. Why? We think this step is a part of forgiveness, rather than repentance. We suppose that we should make restitution to somehow influence or persuade them to forgive us. We also expect others to make restitution to us before we will truly forgive them. Yet, the Scriptures teach that we should simply forgive. Nothing is added to that anywhere in the Bible. So, restitution is really a way of demonstrating true repentance. It may also be a part of the consequences we must accept.

A Typical Scenario

Have you ever had or heard a conversation with someone that went something like this? You or they are mopping the floor and commenting to someone, "This is difficult. I never realized how hard housework can be. Yesterday was a house cleaning day for my wife (husband) and me. To be honest, I really did not want to clean up. So, I got up late and took a really long time getting ready, but that didn't work. When she (he) told me to come and help, we got into an argument. It wasn't long before the conviction of the Holy Spirit came."

"First, I went to God and asked for His forgiveness; then I went to my wife (husband) and humbly asked for her (his) forgiveness, but I couldn't stop there. I felt so sorry, I had to make restitution. So, I am doing yesterday's housework, and then I realized how poorly I had behaved. So, I decided that I would add some extra cleaning to what she (he) wanted me to do, so I am adding two additional things."

A Scriptural Principle

Now we come to our next critical principle of forgiveness. The seventh principle is "we should demonstrate repentance by making restitution." This biblical truth of restitution will involve primarily doing something we should have done, or maybe replacing something we took, lost, or broke, perhaps retracting something we should not have said, or redoing something we should not have done in the first place. This is not penance to make-up for our transgressions, so someone we wronged will forgive us. God does not require this from us because that it is considered "good works." As a result, forgiveness is based on His grace, not any works. We are to forgive one who transgresses us based on God's grace. Then, someone does the same for us. This is God's way.

A Biblical Explanation

Restitution is not a part of the forgiveness process of the person wronged but a part of the repentance process of the person who did the wrong. It is to demonstrate repentance to the wronged party and ourselves. This process may also be a part of the consequences of our wrongdoing and will definitely aid in the repair of a broken relationship. For us to forgive or be forgiven, it is not biblically required. Christians are to forgive whether restitution comes or not. When we are truly sorry for what we did, it is very natural to want to fix the wrong. Sometimes, the person wronged does not require restitution; then it does not have to be done.

In the Old Testament, as the people of Israel journeyed through the wilderness, the Lord was preparing them to be a nation devoted to Him and to His will. He set certain laws that He wanted Israel to follow as His nation and people. These laws were either moral, legal, ceremonial, or even a combination of two or all three. The Lord also determined that different misdeeds, both intentional and unintentional, would have different consequences which depended on the specific actions. Most of these misdeeds involved making restitution to the one transgressed. This was to be done as a manner of life, whether a judgment (legal actions) was given or not (personal actions). In either case, since God was also transgressed a sacrifice had to be made to the priest.

In Leviticus 6:4, God declares, "Then it shall be, if he has sinned, and is guilty, he shall restore that which he took by robbery, or the thing which he has gotten by oppression, or the deposit which was committed to him, or the lost thing which he found." The Lord begins with a list of wrong doing that needs to be recompensed. The most important issue is that it actually occurred. Since these are national laws, then the person needs to be found guilty. If it is a personal act, then the person must admit he did it. This is the confession step we have discussed. Then the Lord God gives a list of infractions and explains exactly what He desires to be done to make restitution for them, "He shall restore it even in full, and shall add a fifth part more to it."

The person who makes restitution should give the same amount back plus twenty percent more. Then God provides the exact timetable for this to occur, "To him to whom it belongs he shall give it, in the day of his being found guilty." As soon as people are found guilty of the transgression or in a personal case admit it, they should begin the restitution process. This demonstrates repentance, the acceptance of the consequences and the desire to restore the relationship. In

Numbers 5:6-7, the Lord God reiterates His commands concerning restitution again. Here God summarizes this important truth. In verse 6, God commands, "Speak to the children of Israel: 'When a man or woman commits any sin that men commit, so as to trespass against Yahweh, and that soul is guilty."

God speaks of every transgression that involves others in anyway which is also a transgression against God. Then He explains what they are to do. In verse 7, God explains, "Then he shall confess his sin which he has done, and he shall make restitution for his guilt in full, and add to it the fifth part of it, and give it to him in respect of whom he has been guilty." Here, God's people were to give back what they took or lost, tell the truth if they had spread lies, and add a fifth part. So, they would add twenty percent more, if possible.

The Old Testament writers provide several examples of restitution. One illustration is the spurning of David by man named Nabal when he would not provide the hospitality that the culture at the time demanded of him. When his wife Abigail asked for forgiveness, she provided restitution. In 1 Samuel 25:27, the author records, "Now this present which your servant has brought to my lord, let it be given to the young men who follow my lord." We discover from 1 Samuel 25:18 the contents of this important "present" was, "Then Abigail hurried and took two hundred loaves of bread, two bottles of wine, five sheep ready dressed, five seahs of parched grain, one hundred clusters of raisins, and two hundred cakes of figs, and laid them on donkeys."

This restitution would have more than provided for all their needs. Also, it built a relationship between Abigail and David that would later blossom into a marriage when she became a widow at God's hand. In 1 Samuel 25:32-33, David responded with this great blessing, "David said to Abigail,

'Blessed is Yahweh, the God of Israel, who sent you today to meet me!'" First, he gives tribute to the Lord then to Abigail. He continues, "Blessed is your discretion, and blessed are you, who have kept me today from blood guiltiness, and from avenging myself with my own hand."

There is no specific command by Jesus Christ or the other inspired writers to make restitution in every instance. Yet, it certainly appears to be a practice in normal Jewish life. The story of the two debtors in Matthew 18:23-35, both offered to make restitution for their debts, though neither was able to. Many are familiar with the story of the repentance of the prodigal son. After this son consumed his portion of the inheritance, even before his father had died, he experienced much grief and sorrow. He then decided that he would return to his loving father and beg for forgiveness and ask if he could be a day laborer to make restitution. Here, Jesus discusses it as a part of normal life.

An Ancient Portrait

The classic biblical example of making restitution is the tax-collector Zacchaeus when he meets Jesus, repents, and receives the Lord. The story of Zacchaeus is found in Luke 19:1-10. Jesus Christ entered the town of Jericho on His way to Jerusalem for the yearly Passover with a large crowd. This important city was on the main route to Jerusalem, and all the pilgrims would be traveling through this town also. The citizens of Jericho would have heard that Jesus had raised Lazarus from the dead and would have come out to see Him. The town would have been teeming with people.

Amid this crowd, a rich and powerful tax collector named Zacchaeus entered the scene. It was the law that once these officials charged the people what Rome had designated, they could then charge any fee they desired. As a result, these men gouged the people and became rich. If they did not pay, the tax collectors would try and intimidate them into paying through threats or physical force. He was one of the "chief" tax collectors, so he also received a percentage of the amount of taxes collected by every tax collector under him. This made him even richer.

They were hated by the Jews because they were extorting the people and working for the Romans. The Hebrews called them "sinners." This was the lowest class of people in their country. They were unclean, defiled, and outcasts. These evil people were to be completely avoided and not allowed to enter the home of a Jew or the synagogue. Zacchaeus was a member of this group. He had heard that the Lord Jesus was in town and wanted to see Him. Why? We can discern this from what happened.

This hated man was honestly seeking true salvation as the Holy Spirit was working powerfully in his heart. The Spirit was convicting Him of His sin and leading Him to the Jesus, the Savior. He had one "big" problem. He was small, a little man vying for a place to see in a large crowd. So, Zacchaeus decided to run ahead of Jesus and find himself a place to see this extraordinary man. He climbed up into a sycamore or perhaps a mulberry tree because these had short trunks and long branches which made them easy to climb. When the Messiah came to the place where Zacchaeus was located, something remarkable happened.

The Lord stopped, looked him straight in the eyes, and called him by his name. Jesus knew Zacchaeus, who he was and all that he had done. He said, "Come down, I will stay with you today." Jesus decided to lodge with him overnight. This tax collector hurried down and received the Lord Jesus joyfully into his home. Zacchaeus stood before Jesus and repented saying, "Behold, Lord, half of my goods I will give to the poor." The Lord Christ's recognition of Zacchaeus was miraculous and obviously the final action that convinced this searching but scorned man that Jesus was the Christ. It obviously led to his act of repentance. In his repentance, we see a very dramatic reaction to receiving Christ as Savior and Lord. Zacchaeus first declares he will give half of his money away. Why? Money had been his idol and his god. Now Jesus was His God and Lord, and he wouldn't serve money any longer.

Then Zacchaeus committed himself to making restitution. This tax collector had essentially stolen and cheated so many people out of so much money that he declared, "If I have wrongfully exacted anything of anyone, I restore four times as much." He saw the awfulness of his greed which had led him to oppress many innocent people and absolutely had to compensate them even more than required. The Lord saw this dramatic response and declared, "Today, salvation has come to this house." This was a true son of Abraham in the Spirit now not one of the flesh alone.

The Lord Jesus doesn't correct Zacchaeus regarding the restitution but affirms it as a demonstration of his strong repentance. Does not restitution make sense in not only displaying one's true repentance but also in rebuilding the broken relationship? It is such a typical occurrence in our lives. If we break someone's stuff, we have it fixed. If we eat someone's pie by mistake, we will replace it. The conscience demands a proper demonstration of repentance through restitution, and this humble action will aid in the crucial process of restoring relationships. It is not commanded in the New Testament, but it was definitely an Old Testament law and pattern. Also, it makes good sense. Sometimes, it is hard to take the necessary steps to make restitution, but we will never be disappointed by its supernatural effects. More importantly, it always demonstrates repentance and honors our glorious Lord.

A Modern Anecdote

We live in a world of credit cards and personal loans. If we so desire, we can simply purchase anything by sliding a card into a machine, and it is ours. Unfortunately, the money must be paid back with interest, and this is a source of much conflict between couples in their marriages. One such couple came to my counseling office to speak about this very issue. From the start, the couple had decided that the wife ought to be a "stay at home mom" and handle the actual payment of the bills while her husband worked. The problem started when her only child, a daughter, entered high school. Before that time, mom was quite involved with her school. When the high school years began, her daughter simply did not want her mother around. The wife suddenly had a large amount of time on her hands. To fill the time, she developed a practice of going shopping. At first, she merely window shopped, but it was not very long before she was noticing the many sales she was missing out on. In fact, she felt like the family was losing money as she perused the sales but did not buy.

So, she decided to utilize the family's credit cards to make the purchases that they needed in order to take advantage of the numerous sales and save money. It soon turned into the things she wanted for herself. Within months, their credit cards were maxed out. At first, she was panicked. Then an idea came to her. She would borrow money from the college savings account earmarked for their daughter and then quickly and quietly pay it back. At first, it started with small withdrawals. Then she didn't have enough to pay for all the credit card minimum payments, and so she had to leave the deficit in the savings. This happened more often than she had anticipated. Over a matter of time, the savings account was depleted, and her daughter's future at college was in jeopardy. It finally came to a head when the daughter asked her father if she could use her college money to hire a tutor to help her prepare for her college entrance exams. Since she would be taking these exams in another year, she wanted to be ready. When her father finally went to the bank to make the appropriate withdrawal, the teller explained to him that he had insufficient funds.

He could not believe what he had just heard. This was impossible, so he demanded to see the bank manager. As she showed him the many withdrawals his wife had made over the past months, the husband squirmed in his seat. After humbly apologizing, the husband drove home furious with his "out of control" wife. He stomped in the house, shouted a series of unflattering and unholy words at her, and then he demanded an explanation. A huge argument ensued. When the teenage daughter found out what her mother had done, she ran into her room and cried about her now grim future. Finally, the wife and mother confessed what she had done. The hard part was actually over, she regretted her actions and desired reconciliation as did her husband and daughter.

Though this is admirable, the wife was not the only one at fault. I gently confronted her husband for not watching over her as Christ does His church. He was too preoccupied with his work schedule to notice even what she had purchased. Her daughter also felt badly because she wouldn't let her mom around the school when that was such an important part of her mother's life. After each had asked the Lord for forgiveness, they turned toward each other and requested forgiveness. As we finished up the wife suddenly said, "I want to get a job and pay the entire college fund back before my daughter needs the money. I want to make restitution!

The husband and the daughter responded with their own desire to help by taking on extra hours and paying off the credit card debt. After some time, everything was restored. I encouraged the mother to take her extra time and use her spiritual gifts to minster to the saints and share the gospel. She now happily works at her local Bible church with young mothers during her free time (Titus 2:3-4). What an amazing supernatural example of making restitution with someone flowing out of deep repentance!

Chapter 8

Accept the Consequences

Another step involves the willingness to accept all the consequences for what we have done. This truth can be seen in various relationships we have. Children living at home will have consequences for violating their parent's rules. At times, our spouses may desire to set up boundaries for some habitual sinful behavior we may have developed during the marriage (drunkenness, drug use, gambling, etc.). They may require us to seek help or take the risk of a break-up of the marriage. These are consequences of our sins.

The church is required to discipline its many members for unrepentant sins against the brethren (Matthew 18:17). We always find that our employers have rules and consequences for breaking them. Every society has a government which creates its laws and punishes its citizens for violating them. Even our friends may have to help us get back in line with them by providing consequences for our behavior towards them. In fact, every healthy relationship has boundaries and rules set up formally or informally with consequences for ones who refuse to respect the other member or members. God may intervene and have consequences of His own since we have also violated His laws. This chapter involves the discussion of these consequences and their importance.

A Typical Scenario

Imagine yourself involved in an intense time-consuming activity. You suddenly look at your clock, gasp, and scream, "Oh no, I forgot to pick up (insert name) at their activity. He (she) is going to be so angry at me. I came into the family room to retrieve my keys and had just a few extra minutes. Then I got started, and those minutes turned into an hour. I totally forgot to pick (insert name) up!" Suddenly, your flesh begins to flare up, and you think, "I'm in trouble, but I don't care. That is not my problem! Everybody makes mistakes. If I get the silent treatment or yelled at, then I will give it back to him (her)" Has this ever happened to you? It has to me. Sometimes, we do something wrong, but we refuse to accept the consequences. This is not what God desires.

A Scriptural Principle

We now come to principle number eight. This principle is "we should accept whatever consequences that may result from our sin against God and others." Sin leads to a variety of consequences. When we travel back to the garden, God told Adam that if he disobeyed Him and ate of a particular tree, he would die. That is a consequence of sin. When Adam ate of the fruit, he died, not physically but spiritually and set in motion a myriad of consequences for that one act.

A Biblical Explanation

Why must there be consequences to almost everything we do? Scientists describe it as a simple case of cause and effect. To every action there is some kind of reaction or effect. The Bible describes it as a law of God set forth in His universe. In Galatians 5, Paul had just contrasted the fruits of the Spirit with the deeds of the flesh. In Galatians 6, to encourage the saints at Galatia to remain diligent in producing these fruits (doing good), he explains that the spiritual realm functions according to this cause-and-effect relationship. In verses 7-8, he utilizes a farming analogy to explain it. He writes, "Don't be deceived. God is not mocked, for whatever a man sows, that he will also reap. For he who sows to his own flesh will from the flesh reap corruption. But he who sows to the Spirit will from the Spirit reap eternal life."

Here the apostle describes a general principle of farming. If a farmer sows with good seeds, he will reap good crops; if he sows using bad seeds, he will reap bad crops. Whatever he sows, he will reap. Then Paul explains how this physical analogy applies to supernatural things. When Christians sin by sowing to the flesh, they reap corruption. When believers live righteously and sow to the Spirit, they reap eternal life. When we follow our lusts, they lead us to corrupt activities, not activities of eternal life. When we follow the Spirit, He leads us to activities having to do with eternal life.

In our seeking forgiveness context, we have sown bad seeds into our relationships with people, and now we must reconcile with them. Since we sowed bad seed into the relationship, there will come some bad consequences. When we repent of the sin, we should still expect some of those consequences. This is most often in the form of restitution. We may have to retract something we should not have said, do something we did not do, undo something we did, fix what we broke or even replace what we lost. Accepting these consequences demonstrates our repentance also. So, restitution could be one of the many ways we accept the consequences for our sins against others.

Another way we might have to accept the consequences for our sin is to allow the people transgressed to deal with our sin in the manner and time frame they may require, not the manner and time frame we may require. For example, if we make our spouses, parents, friends, neighbors, children, fellow students, or co-workers angry and they ignore us for a few days, we must accept this consequence for our action.

They could need time to work out their responses to our sinful actions. If we violate a trust of our parents or spouses, we may have to check in with them more often. Perhaps, they will want everything we say to be verified for a while. These consequences ought to be accepted. It might not be something we might think they should need to rebuild the trust, but they do.

The third reason accepting consequences is so critical to a relationship is that this is God's basic strategy to train us. If we refuse to accept the consequences for our sins, we are circumventing our learning process. Because God is a loving Father, He trains and disciplines us to act like Him and live in a holy way. This is called "sanctification." Accepting the many consequences for our actions will assist in the training process. In Hebrews 12:7, speaking of the numerous trials in the life of believers, the author declares, "It is for discipline that you endure. God deals with you as with children, for what son is there whom his father doesn't discipline?"

God brings trials into the lives of His children (some self-imposed) to train them. This is what a loving father will do. The Greek word translated "discipline" means "instruction, learning, teaching, or training." Then in verse 8, the author continues, "But if you are without discipline, of which all have been made partakers, then are you illegitimate, and not children." True believers are always disciplined by their Father. People who claim that they are Christians but are never disciplined for their sin cannot be true children of God. Then in verse 10, the author says, "For they indeed, for a few days, punished us as seemed good to them." Earthly fathers discipline us for a few days to help us be good in this life, but God has something greater in mind. He adds, "But he for our profit, that we may be partakers of his holiness." God trains His children to partake of His own holiness. We are provided this chance though His discipline process.

In verse 11, the inspired writer asserted, "All chastening seems for the present to be not joyous, but grievous." We do not like God's discipline. It can be extremely unpleasant. Yet, the results are so powerful. He finishes, "Yet afterward it yields the peaceful fruit of righteousness to those who have been exercised thereby." The training is for righteous living which brings forth peace. In our context, it is the peace we will have in our relationships. How do the consequences of our actions fit into God's discipline? The consequences for actions are often the very discipline God uses to keep us on the right path. The consequences make us say to ourselves, "I better not do that again. That was too painful! I never want to experience that again!"

As with restitution, accepting the consequences of our sins is a part of the repentance process and not forgiveness. The people we have wronged should forgive us whether we decide to accept the consequences or not. But like restitution, it does demonstrate to them that we are repentant. Also, it helps to rebuild the relationship. It is not penance for sin nor is it works for our own forgiveness from Him or those we have transgressed. This is an important difference.

At times, God might use the government to intervene in our dispute. When a wrong is done to another and is against the law, whether we repent or not, there will still come some kind of consequences. In Romans 13:1-4, Paul indicates that the government is the arm of God to provide consequences for grievous sins. In verse four Paul explains, "For he is a servant of God to you for good. But if you do that which is evil, be afraid, for he doesn't bear the sword in vain; for he is a servant of God, an avenger for wrath to him who does evil." To learn from their mistakes, the saints must take the punishment that the law demands. This again demonstrates their repentance toward God and the party wronged. If one ignores them, how can one demonstrate repentance?

It is important to understand that sometimes God will not use natural consequences for sin but deal directly with His children. There are numerous examples of this in both the Old and New Testaments. For example, the leader of Israel, Moses, was not allowed to enter the Promised Land because he struck the rock two times while he rebuked the people in anger. This was in direct defiance of the Lord's command (Numbers 20:9-12). David lost his son from his adulterous relationship with Bathsheba and his murder of her husband Uriah (2 Samuel 12).

There were many saints at Corinth who were sick due to their improper observance of communion (1 Corinthians 11:30). Since God does not speak to us directly any longer, He may bring a trial from some kind of odd circumstances or perhaps one that seems like it came out of nowhere to get our attention. When this occurs, we should ask ourselves if we are in the midst of committing a sin which God wants stopped. So, it is important to accept the consequences of sin.

An Ancient Portrait

A great example of the acceptance of the consequences for one's sins in a relationship is found in a parable told by our Lord in Luke 15:17-31. This is the tale of the Prodigal Son. In this story a son rebels against his father, repents, and is then restored based on the father's love and grace, not the son's works. The Pharisees saw God as accepting only those who had a righteousness from good works, rather than faith. It did not matter the evil that was in their hearts. Jesus told this tale to demonstrate that God will seek out even the outcasts of this world, call them, forgive them, and accept them into His kingdom apart from works. The heart is what matters. Though this is the intent of this story, it also teaches other principles such as accepting consequences for sins.

A certain man had two sons. The younger son demanded from his father all of his inheritance. In that culture, he was essentially saying that he wished his dad was dead, so he could cash him out. The father should have slapped him in the face, dismissed him from the family, and treated him as dead. The town would then rebuke, scorn, and shun him for such disrespectful behavior. This would have been a typical Jewish response. Instead, the father breaks with all forms of tradition and gives him one-third of all he had. This was the younger son's portion (Deuteronomy 21:17).

The father would remain in the full management of the property until his death. His son could sell his portion, but the buyer would have to wait until the owner (father) died to collect. It would be a future investment for a buyer. The first-born son would manage the property and then retain the rights to the remaining two-thirds which were not sold. This was the ancient custom for handling inheritance and property.

The son cashed out and took off to a very distant Gentile country. It was a place where he would not be known, and it would be inhabited by citizens who would not even know his traditions or customs of behavior. Also, these non-Jewish citizens would be very unfamiliar with either His God or His God's laws. This way, he was absolutely free to behave any way that he desired. He proceeded to waste all of his money. He squandered assets that had been passed down from one generation to another in his family on riotous living. He had committed all the sins that money could buy. He spent and spent while he partied and partied until it was all gone. He consumed everything until he was left with nothing.

For the first time in his life, he became virtually penniless and utterly destitute. Then a famine came, and there was no food in the land. Everyone was starving, including him. So, this impoverished son decided to attach himself (Jesus uses the word "glued") to a citizen of the land. This term "citizen" would have meant that he was a man of means, and yet he did not have much interest in helping him. This is why the son ended up in the rich man's field feeding the pigs. A good Jewish boy could not eat or even touch the carcass of such an unclean animal (Deuteronomy 14:8; Leviticus 11:7). This was a fitting place to end such an epic episode of one man's rebellion. Yet, Jesus describes how he found God. It is often out of some deep desperation that we turn back to God. The amazing thing is that He truly welcomes us as this father did his son.

As he was feeding the pigs, he began to desire the pods that the pigs were eating. He was so hungry that this now crazed son literally fought the pigs for their left-over food. No one was available to help him get it. In the midst of this terrible condition of chaos and dying of starvation, he came to his senses. He woke up from his sinful stupor and took a hard look at his predicament. He had gotten himself into a huge mess. Then his heart changed, and the son completely repented. Obviously, he confessed his wickedness, mourned over the evil he had done, and turned from his sins; this is implied. The rebellious son decided that he ought to return home and declare to his father that he had sinned against heaven and him. He knew that he was not worthy to be his father's son; instead, he would beg to be a day-laborer.

The point of requesting to be a day-laborer indicated the son's intent to pay back the entire amount he had spent, no matter how long it took. Not only was he willing to make restitution but willing to accept the consequences of his sin, even if it meant holding the lowest position on the estate. Even the slaves had shelter and food. All he would receive was perhaps a job every day, if there was work available. To return, the son would also have to face the consequence of shame and humiliation from the townspeople, his father, and his older brother. He did not care. He would accept and bare it all. He would not attempt to dodge, guilt his father into removing, or even brow beat him into rescinding the humiliating outcome of his foolish and impulsive actions. He had to learn from his mistakes. As he approached the town, the father had been waiting for him. He ran swiftly to his son and hugged him, kissed him, and also forgave him.

Most know the rest of the story. The son was not required to do restitution or bare any of the consequences of his sin except for the starvation of the famine. This was solved by his loving father who provided a magnificent feast for him. Perhaps, if Jesus Christ was teaching on the importance of accepting the consequences of his sin, the outcome might have been quite different. Jesus is teaching the Pharisees the absolute free gift of eternal life without works, so the father had to offer all to the son because that is what God does at salvation. We will look at the rest of the story in another part of the book. As we can see so clearly from the son's behavior, accepting the consequences is a part of our repentance. Whether we must humbly make the restitution or suffer the consequences is up to the person wronged, the governing authorities, or even God. Yet, we must be willing to accept every consequence that may arise.

A Modern Anecdote

One day, two male friends came into my office obviously upset with one another. They explained that normally they would not think this was a matter for counseling, but their college pastor referred them to me. He knew that they had been best friends since the first grade, and he did not want them to lose the relationship they had. Everyone watched them grow up together in the church and wanted them to reconcile. After a few sessions, I discovered that they were attending college together and shared an apartment. Since Steve's parents were willing to co-sign on the apartment, it was in his name alone.

Every month, John would pay his friend Steve half of the rent and utilities in cash, and Steve would pay the bills. Then one day, John came home to see a sign posted on the front door indicating that they were being evicted. This occurred because Steve had not paid three month's rent. Of course, John blew up and started shouting at Steve. He demanded to know exactly what had happened. His roommate could not understand how Steve could not have paid the rent since his parents were supporting him, while John had to work. Steve began with a long list of pathetic excuses, but none of them were adequate to explain why the rent wasn't paid.

Finally, John gave up and went downstairs and paid the three month's rent. Six months later, the same thing occurred again. Steve had the same litany of excuses with no real reason for not paying the rent. He had now had enough and was going to move out and never speak to Steve again. It was time for a closer examination of the facts. It turns out that Steve had always been irresponsible. Since John liked Steve so much, he simply ignored it for so long that John almost became unaware of it.

Steve had low grades, was always fooling around in school, missed his SAT's three times, couldn't hold down a decent job, and finally got into college because his dad knew someone who knew someone. When they were younger, every time they went over to Steve's house, his parents would complain about his poor grades and lazy behavior but never did anything. He had never been disciplined, and John knew that one day Steve's nonsense would catch up to him too. What John did not anticipate (and should have) was that Steve would be involved when it finally happened. It was explained to John that it was finally time for Steve to accept consequences for his actions or he would never learn to take responsibility.

This did not mean the drastic measure of destroying their friendship over it. It did mean that John would have to move out and find another roommate, and let Steve learn from his mistakes. Before he did that, John thought he should give Steve one more chance, by having him put three month's rent in a savings account with John's name on it in case this were to happen again. In the Old Testament, the Lord God gave Israel so many warnings and opportunities, before He judged them.

As a result, John should give Steve one final chance. If it happens again, he should close the savings account, pay the back rent and move out. All of the other aspects of their relationship could remain in place; they simply could not become financially dependent on one another again. I told him, he should sit Steve down and explain all of this to him in a calm manner. The Lord God has set consequences into place to help define relationships and build them. Once the pressure was off John, he could finally enjoy the friendship they had as kids. It is important that we are not constantly bailing people out of their self-imposed problems because of "love."

Believers must allow people to accept the consequences of their mistakes and sins in order for them to learn from them. This is the way of God. This is one of the loving methods our Father uses to discipline us as His children. This is even the way a loving human father behaves. It is the basic blueprint for the raising of human children and the raising of God's children.

Chapter 9

Gently Confront Sin

In the last chapter, we discussed the gentle confrontation of sin. We must confront those who have sinned against us. This would occur after we had asked them for forgiveness even if they started the conflict. This was the last step in that process. We also viewed the gentle confrontation of sin as the initial step in when others have transgressed us. After this, the action that should be taken by all Christians should be to forgive as they are forgiven.

A Typical Scenario

Have you ever had or heard a conversation with a spouse, parent, or friend about your neighbor that went something like this? You say or hear (holding a torn dress shirt in your hand), "I have had it with that neighbor! Every discussion we have gets ugly. There will be no more arguments about who was the greatest president ever to serve. We both got angry, I threw a soda in his face, and he ripped this shirt. I am going over there right now to give him a large piece of my mind for ruining my good clothes. (Pause for a thought.) Wait! I cannot possibly behave that way. It will utterly ruin my relationship with him. He is my friend! Besides, I bear responsibility also. I need to go over and apologize.

In this simple illustration both parties bear responsibility for transgressing their relationship. Usually, one will begin a problem with a sinful word or action, then another responds sinfully and then they go back and forth. This destroys many relationships. Both are required to ask for forgiveness for the sins they committed. They must leave the response of the other to God. We ask and leave it up to God to prompt the other to ask also. Then, we graciously accept it.

A Scriptural Principle

The next principle that must guide our reconciliation with others will address both of these common occurrences (final step and the first step) which demand a gentle confrontation. Principle nine is "we must gently confront those who have sinned against us." The definition that I will use for the word "confront" in our discussion will be this: to face people and explain exactly what they did wrong. It will not include its usual negative connotation of hostility.

This is a time of mutual information exchange, not a time of bitter and angry confrontation. We explain our motives and reasons for what we did and then give them a chance to explain theirs. We may describe what we think are their transgressions, and they may add our own transgressions to the discussion. We attempt to discover exactly what actually happened, not what we think may have happened. This is a time devoted to clearing things up.

A Biblical Explanation

To gently confront sin is the final step in reconciling with those we have transgressed. It is the first step in reconciling with others who have transgressed us. Let's face it, in most conflicts we both will bear responsibility for the many evil words spoken and actions taken. We may have more or less responsibility, or an equal amount. At times, one party may have no responsibility. In any of these cases, we are required by our Lord to go and reconcile the relationship. If we have sinned in any way, we must ask for forgiveness. Once it is granted, then we should gently confront them concerning their part in the problem. If we do not feel we have sinned, then we must approach them with a gentle confrontation. This step will also allow them to confront us, in case we are unaware of our sin.

When a transgression occurs, people usually wait for the other to approach them. Jesus does not provide this option for the people of His kingdom. Instead, in Matthew 5:23-24, Jesus proclaimed, "If therefore you are offering your gift at the altar, and there remember that your brother has anything against you, leave your gift there before the altar, and go your way. First be reconciled to your brother, and then come and offer your gift." Notice, the Lord Jesus said that if others have something against us, we are to go to them, not if we have something against them. Notice also, the Lord does not say that if someone has something against us and we bear most of the responsibility for what happened, then we ought to go. He did not assign any weight of responsibility or guilt to the person who was to go. If we have any responsibility, we are to go.

On certain occasions, we may actually think that we bear no responsibility for any sin in the conflict; then, we should go to them and gently confront their sin against us. This is the first step in handling all those who transgress us. In Matthew 18:15. Jesus declares, "If your brother sins against you, go, show him his fault between you and him alone. If he listens to you, you have gained back your brother." If we do not go to confront them, they may not even know there is a problem.

This confrontation has several critical purposes. First, it provides an opportunity to discuss the facts and come to an agreement as to what actually happened. Sometimes, the message we send in our words and actions are not really what we may have intended. Other times, we think we said something that may have been in our minds but was not actually spoken. Often, in the heat of the moment we think someone said or did something when they did not. We are fallible and get things mixed up. This process allows a time for figuring out exactly what was said and done.

We can discern what message was sent and how each felt about it. This provides a great opportunity to share feelings. When feelings are aroused, they cannot simply be dismissed. Also, we are a product of all of our various experiences. Therefore, a word or action may mean one thing to us and a very different thing to others. These meanings produce very powerful emotions. Because they are not our feelings, we may dismiss them. This destroys relationships. Our lives, views, values, and feelings are not the only valid ones. Our partners have lives, views, values, and feelings that are also valid. These must be communicated and acknowledged by both parties, especially when they are different. This gentle confrontation process will allow this kind of communication to occur.

The second purpose is that it allows us to repent of our sins. Once the facts are clearly seen, responsibility can be taken, and repentance will follow. Third, it allows others to repent of their sins. God desires this repentance. Fourth, it provides the opportunity to reconcile and "gain back" the relationship with a fellow believer. In the end of Matthew 18:15, Jesus explains the purpose, "If he listens to you, you have gained back your brother." The relationship will be rebuilt and restored. Fifth, it allows an unbeliever to repent of the sin and perhaps receive Jesus as Savior and Lord. Is not the confrontation of sin an essential part of the gospel message (Romans 1:18; 3:23)? Is it supposed to be sort of a generic sin message or can it deal with specific sins? In Acts

2:23, Peter indicted the Jews for crucifying Jesus. That is very specific. In Acts 7:52-53, Stephen spoke specifically of the transgressions of the Jewish leaders: killing the prophets, the Righteous One (Jesus), and refusing to obey God's law.

Sixth, it helps Christians escape from the snare of the Devil. In 2 Timothy 2:24-26, Paul writes, "The Lord's servant must not quarrel, but be gentle towards all, able to teach, patient, in gentleness correcting those who oppose him." Here, Timothy is encouraged to correct those who oppose him. Then, Paul explains the reason for this, "Perhaps God may give them repentance leading to a full knowledge of the truth, and they may recover themselves [come to their senses and escape] out of the devil's snare [trap], having been taken captive by him to do his will." Notice, the apostle explains to Timothy that his correction will lead to these true believers escaping the snare and trap that the Devil had them in. The Devil can capture Christians into a wrong kind of thinking which can destroy many of their relationships.

This time of confrontation must be done in gentleness. It is not an angry or bitter engagement. In Galatians 6:1, Paul explains that Christians must restore in a spirit of gentleness. There is no actual time frame or statute of limitations for this process of gentle confrontation. If someone has wronged us in the past, we can still go years later and gently confront them or ask for forgiveness to heal the wounds in our own life and theirs.

As a counselor, I often suggest that my clients work out issues with parents or children even though many if not all the transgressions may have occurred years, perhaps many years, before. The wounds from our past are still there and affect our lives in the present time. There is no statute of limitations on gentle confrontation. It can be done at any time in the future. This will also aid in the healing process.

An Ancient Portrait

The proper and improper steps of this gentle confronting of sin are illustrated through the interaction of two sisters, Martha and Mary with Jesus. This is found in Luke 10:38-42. While Jesus was out preaching the gospel, He decided to stay the night at their house. You can imagine how excited the sisters would be, but both had very different reactions. Once Martha welcomed Jesus into her home, Mary parked herself right next to Jesus and began to listen to Him teach.

Luke recorded that Mary sat at the feet of Jesus and heard His word. Sitting at a person's feet was an expression that meant to get as close as you can to hear them as they spoke. The Greek word translated "heard" means more than just hearing someone speak, but it would include "attending to, attempting to understand, and considering what is being said." In the Greek, the tense of this verb is in the imperfect active indicative demonstrating a continuous action in past time. Mary was listening as the Lord was speaking. This was the Lord of all teaching truth, and she was learning.

But where was Mary's sister? Why wasn't she also sitting at the feet of our Lord Jesus? What was Martha doing? She was attempting to serve the Lord by preparing a fine meal for him. Unlike Mary, Martha was working in the kitchen. Luke described her as "distracted with much serving." The Greek word translated "serving" is the word for "ministry" in the New Testament. Martha was ministering to the Lord in a different way. Mary's sister was ministering to the Lord by handling all the preparations for His stay. What a selfless and wonderful act of kindness. Then she got "distracted" by it. The Greek word which is translated "distracted" means "dragged away with, over-occupied, too busy with." She got dragged away with the work, and it suddenly had become overwhelming. Why? Luke explains that there were "much" preparations. Perhaps, she intended to put something nice together but not too elaborate. Then she got carried away, and suddenly there seemed to be so much to do. So, the task got bigger and bigger in her mind. Allowing Mary to sit and listen to the Lord seemed fine at first, but now the entire thing became too much for one human being to handle.

Then she had really had enough. Martha was in the other room while Mary was enjoying the time with Jesus, and she was missing out! Luke writes that she "came up" to Jesus. The Greek word translated "came up" means "to come up and stand over." The Lord would have been seated in a place of honor outside in the home's courtyard (like our backyard patio). Mary would have been seated in front of Him, rather than to the side. She was listening. There most likely would have been other guests who had come to hear Jesus. In the midst of this, Martha just marches right in and would have stopped any conversation.

Standing over the both of them, obviously like an enraged mother whose children had made a mess, they needed to clean up; she began to let the Lord have it! She doesn't even talk to Mary but goes right to the top. She chastises the Lord for allowing Mary to get out of all the work and leave her stuck with the preparations. Martha scolds, "Lord, don't you care that my sister left me to serve alone?" Martha accuses the Lord of being insensitive to her problems and showing favoritism to her sister. This is the Master of the universe. Couldn't Jesus see how stressed, upset, and overwhelmed she was with everything? Doesn't He care about her?

Here Martha accuses her sister Mary indirectly of leaving her alone to serve Jesus. The Greek word translated "left" means "to leave or to abandon." Martha felt abandoned by her sibling Mary and completely alone. Then after accusing Jesus of such an insensitive act, her audaciousness continues.

Then Martha directs, "Ask her therefore to help me." This sister of Mary basically demanded the Lord to command Mary to help her. Actually, Martha does the right thing, only in the wrong way. The woman felt wronged, and according to Matthew 18:15, what should she have done? She should have gently confronted the sins. That part was righteous and according to biblical principles. All the rest went wrong.

First, a gentle confrontation implies that one is not angry. We cannot be gentle and angry at the same time. Remember our use of the word "confront." Martha was not "facing the person and dealing with the issue;" but rather, she dealt with the problem in a very argumentative and hostile manner. Second, we are to go to them privately, not in front of others or to the authority over them. Third, we're to go with the intention of restoring a relationship, not to incite more anger and destroy what we had. Martha should have come up to her sister and excused herself. Then she should have asked to speak to Mary in private having a gentle smile of an intent which would encourage restoration. This is not how Martha behaved, but it is how the Lord Jesus behaved in his response to her. Since she made a public remark, here was a great learning opportunity for all from the master teacher.

Then Jesus responds with a gentle confrontation to restore the relationship with Him first, "Martha, Martha, you are anxious and troubled about so many things." He repeats her name to indicate the utter importance of what He was about to say. He does recognize how upset she is. The language Jesus utilizes indicates that Martha was not just anxious but overly concerned about this problem. Martha was not only troubled but in an uproar. There was much turbulence and great noise in her declaration. Martha's mind had become completely flooded with so many thoughts that she was just acting on impulse. Have you ever been that way? Then Jesus calmly says, "But one thing is needed. Mary has chosen the good part, which will not be taken away from her." The Lord told her that Mary was not going into the kitchen. Martha's service was appreciated, but her sister's learning from the Lord was much more important. It would last into eternity.

Jesus makes a simple point: learning Bible truth is more important than Christian service. We need the truth because it lasts. The word translated "good" here means "the most excellent part, the best part." Service is great also, but it doesn't last. Both are essential, but truth comes first. What a beautiful true story of struggle to confront sin in a gentle way. This is not easy to do as Martha experienced and will require supernatural strength from the Holy Spirit. At times, we may want to confront sin in an argumentative and angry way as Martha did, even using the Bible as a weapon (as Martha wanted to use Jesus). Instead, we need to make our confrontation of sin gentle as Jesus did when He gave His response to Martha. It must also be in private.

A Modern Anecdote

One of the issues people have been dealing with in recent years has been an issue around their consumption of food. I received a phone call from a woman who claimed that her daughter was a Christian and needed help quickly. She had lost a lot of weight and was disappearing right before her eyes. Finally, she noticed that her daughter would eat and then immediately use the bathroom. One day, this mother listened through the door and heard the purging. She was frantic. The young lady came into my office looking gaunt and tired. I discovered that her older sister had criticized her from the time she could remember. It was always the same subject: her weight. She would constantly tell her she needed to lose weight. This produced so much anxiety in her life that she ate even more to relieve it.

She explained that her parents were always working, and so her older sister became her "mother." When she was about seventeen, she became very sick and lost a large amount of weight. The "plump" had finally left her. Suddenly, the boys began to notice her and were calling and texting her all the time. Even some of the girls in her school, who would never even look at her, started talking to her. She became popular and happy. Then the unexpected happened, she began to worry about her weight for the first time in her life. Once her appetite returned, she fell into her old eating habit that put the weight on in the first place: fast food. She adored it.

Rather than give up the fast food, she simply ate as much as she wanted and then went into the restroom and threw it up. She got the idea from a movie she had seen. At first it was disgusting, but she quickly got used to it. She thought this would be the best of both worlds. She could eat as much as she wanted and still remain slim. Eventually, the more that she ate, the more she worried about getting fat. The more she worried about getting fat, the more she ate. Now fast food was all that she ever thought about, and she was constantly tired.

This went on for quite some time. Now she was almost twenty-two, living at home, working for her favorite fast-food restaurant, dating boys, and being tired. She felt stuck in this dilemma. In this situation we took a two-pronged approach. First, we would work on her self-esteem and food problems. To do this, we would begin with her sister whose criticism started this whole issue in the first place. I told her that it was time that she let Jesus be her Lord (Master) and not herself, her sister, fast food, fatigue, or boys. She needed to begin to see herself, not as her sister or the society at large saw her, but how God saw her. Then she had to put away these old habits and put on the utterly new habits that Christ desired. It took many sessions and hard work to get her back on the road to good health and a life that truly glorified her Savior Jesus Christ. Her joy and sense of purpose returned.

The final task was to reconcile the relationships with her family. She called her older sister and asked to meet. When they met, she explained what had been happening to her and how God was working miraculously in her life. The next time they met, she explained what her older sister had done and its contribution to the weight problem. The older sister sat there speechless. She had been so young her- self and had so much responsibility.

The older sister told her that she did not even realize she had hurt her. She sobbed and told her younger sister how sorry she was. She was so glad that this was shared with her so she could repent. Then they hugged and looked forward to a closer relationship in the future. The sister was provided the opportunity to repent and did.

After this, the younger sister also gently confronted her parents who had given so much responsibility to her older sister. They had forced a young girl into being a mother far too early making her words far too important. Of course, they repented. Finally, the younger daughter was confronted for not handling the situation in a healthy, righteous, and holy way. This too was met with confession, sorrow, and repentance by the daughter. This becomes such a beautiful example of a gentle confrontation and how it can reconcile and restore relationships. After this, the young lady was able to move out and begin her future with her relationships in her family now rebuilt. What a powerful testimony of God's power and the importance of a gentle confrontation.

Chapter 10

Forgive as Forgiven

One of the most important steps in forgiveness must be to fully forgive as one is forgiven. As the saints engage in this healing process, they must be willing to forgive all people of all sin they may have done against them. This will not be easy and is a supernatural, divine act. It is important to note that this forgiveness is not dependent on others asking for the forgiveness first, or the acceptance of the consequences. True believers must forgive other believers as the Lord God has forgiven them.

A Typical Scenario

Have you ever had or heard a conversation with a spouse, parent, or friend about a co-worker that went something like this? You say, "I cannot believe he stole my idea at work. I came up with the basic concept of the new company logo and showed it to him. He went to our boss and said it was his. I am so angry. If he ever comes to me and begs for my forgiveness, I'm not forgiving him. He can crawl on his hands and knees, but it will not do any good."

This simple scenario illustrates the fact that sometimes, we do not want to forgive others for what they have done to us. Sometimes the transgression is so hurtful that it becomes difficult to overcome. Other times, we will not forgive out of pure pride or stubbornness. Though He understands that it may take time, He desires that we forgive. If we refuse, this does not sit well with our Lord. He forgives us all that we do every day, and He requires His children to act like Him.

A Scriptural Principle

The next principle in the forgiveness process is principle ten. It is "we must forgive others as we have been forgiven." This principle encompasses several important aspects. First, we must forgive all transgressions, nothing can be held back. Second, we must forgive all people, no one can be excluded. Third, we must forgive all the sins of all the people because we have been forgiven all our sins. Why are we to do this? The primary reason is that God expects His children to behave like Him. Since He has forgiven all the transgressions of believers, so they are to do the same.

A Biblical Explanation

God does not make any distinctions in forgiveness when it comes to His people. All are forgiven. One of the issues that Paul encountered in the churches was a distinction the Christians were making among themselves. Since the Jews were originally God's people, they thought they were above the Gentiles. Paul spent so much time explaining to both groups, God does not make distinctions among people when it comes to His forgiveness and blessings. In Ephesians 3:6, Paul discloses, "That the Gentiles are fellow heirs, and fellow members of the body, and fellow partakers of his promise in Christ Jesus through the Good News." Then in Galatians 3:28, the apostle speaks against other distinctions, "There is neither Jew nor Greek, there is neither slave nor free man, there is neither male nor female; for you are all one in Christ Jesus." All people are forgiven; differences do not matter.

If all believers should be forgiven their sins without any distinctions made, what about unbelievers? Should we make any distinctions among those who do not know Jesus Christ concerning forgiveness? The answer is found in the answer

102

to another question, "Does God call all people to salvation and forgiveness?" In 1 Timothy 2:3, Paul entreated Timothy, his son in the faith, to pray for the salvation of all people, He wrote, "For this is good and acceptable in the sight of God our Savior." Then in verse 4, Paul provided the important reason, "Who desires all people to be saved and come to full knowledge of the truth." So, we must forgive all people.

There were some people mocking believers because they were claiming that Christ was coming back, and He had not yet come. In 2 Peter 3:9, Peter proclaimed, "The Lord is not slow concerning his promise, as some count slowness; but is patient with us, not wishing that any should perish, but that all should come to repentance." Our God desires all people to find forgiveness in His only Son. He does not make any distinctions. This means that the Father desires His children in the same way to also forgive people their transgressions. We cannot say, "He's an unbeliever or (insert some criticism here), and I will not forgive him." The Lord Jesus taught the following principle throughout His ministry. If God forgives the sins of all of us against Him, then we are to forgive the sins against us. In Matthew 6:12, during the Sermon on the Mount, the Lord Jesus explained that the prayers of God kingdom people should conclude with these words, "Forgive us our debts, as we also forgive our debtors."

In Mark 11:25, on His way to Jerusalem, Jesus told His disciples, "Whenever you stand praying, forgive, if you have anything against anyone." In Luke 11:4, when He was asked how to pray, Jesus Christ delivered the Lord's Prayer for a second time which included instruction on the forgiveness of others. He taught His disciples this, "Forgive us our sins, for we ourselves also forgive everyone who is indebted to us." Notice, there are no distinctions made by the Lord Jesus between the saved and the unsaved. He uses the inclusive terms, "debtors," "anyone," and "everyone."

Now, how does this work in real life? When we become filled with anger and bitterness and unwilling to forgive, we must consider the amount and extent of the transgressions we have committed against God. He has made absolutely no distinctions in forgiving us. Then we will discover that the sins against us will look so much smaller in comparison to our large number of sins against God. After this, our hearts will be opened to His Spirit through this biblical truth. Then God's mercy, grace, and love that was shown and is shown every day to us in forgiveness, will pour forth into our own love, grace, and mercy in forgiveness toward others. People struggle with forgiveness when they forget how much they have been forgiven. Sometimes, they may be too proud to realize what horrible sinners they are!

When believers are continually coming before the throne of God begging God for forgiveness, they will understand be able to forgive in a greater way whether the transgressors are believers or not. One of the primary ways Christians can have growing relationships with spouses, parents, children, friends, church members, co-workers, fellow students, and acquaintances is through this constant confession process. We admit our sins, accept His forgiveness, and then provide the same toward all others.

Also, the forgiveness of others does not necessarily occur after we gently confront them with their sin, and they ask for forgiveness. It could happen as the sin is occurring or even immediately afterward. Every sin someone might commit against us cannot possibly be confronted. There are simply too many annoyances and little sins. God certainly does not confront us on every sin we commit, nor does He discipline us. We cannot wait for those who have sinned against us to ask for forgiveness because often they do not or will not. The forgiveness of others is never dependent on their response. This is such an important understanding.

An Ancient Portrait

This principle is beautifully illustrated in the "Parable of the Unforgiving Debtor" in Matthew 18:23-35. Peter had just inquired of the Lord as to whether seven times is enough to forgive someone who had sinned against us. To him that seemed pretty reasonable. To Jesus, it was absurd. Instead, Jesus told him it was more like "seventy times seven." This meant as many times as needed. Then to help His disciples understand the absolute importance of forgiving others as many times as they sin against them, He tells this story.

Jesus begins the story by describing a king who desired to settle accounts with his servants. These were not his slaves in chains but probably provincial governors. They were to pay the king his legal share of their tax revenue in order to support the kingdom. This king discovered that one of his "servants" owed him ten thousand talents. To owe him this much, the governor would have to have kept back the owed tax revenues for many years. It became an impossible sum to pay back. In modern terms, we would owe back taxes, so large that we could not pay them back no matter how long we worked. This man was in a difficult predicament.

The tax revenue of Judea and Samaria together was only two to perhaps three hundred talents, so one can imagine the enormous sum that ten thousand would be. The point is simple: it was an impossible sum to ever pay back. When the king discovered the discrepancy, he would have known that the servant had been cheating the king for a very long time. This would have made him extremely angry. Since he obviously couldn't pay, the king ordered him to be sold into slavery with his whole family. Then whatever he owned would be sold, so some payment could be made. This would come nowhere near the amount owed, but the king would take everything he had and more if possible.

To take all that the man owned and to sell his family into slavery would never earn the king enough to compensate for all the man had stolen. It would cost the servant everything that he had and beyond. This was a common practice among the nations in the ancient world. Everyone who heard Jesus would understand what was described. So, this official fell to the ground in submission and worship and began to beg for mercy from the king. He cried, "Please, please, be patient, and I will repay you!" This would have been impossible, and they both knew it but crying out for the king's patience and mercy was his only hope.

He did not deny his sin or question the king's judgment. He pleaded for mercy! Suddenly, this king felt compassion for the man and released him from the debt. He could have lambasted him for such a ridiculous request, but he did not. He bestowed complete forgiveness on the man and wiped away his debts. The official walked away a free man and unencumbered from any transgressions. He had pleaded for mercy and received it. Does this not sound like believers who plead for mercy, receive Christ as Savior and Lord, and are released from all the debts of their sin? Yes, it does, and this is the first point Christ is making to Peter.

Then, something utterly hypocritical happened. The man immediately proceeded to behave in a way that was almost exactly opposite of the forgiveness the king had shown him. Obviously, while he was trembling before the patient king, he must have remembered that someone else should actually be trembling before him. Once released, the official decided to search for the man who had owed him some money, and he would not receive the same kind of mercy from him. He did not care that in comparison to the debt that was just forgiven; it was a small amount of only one hundred denarii. When he found him, he grabbed him by the throat since the debtor was on the same level as him (a fellow servant).

Since this debtor was referred to as "fellow servant," he would have been on the same level as the first one. These men knew each other well. While the first servant's hands were wrapped around his throat choking him, the official demanded payment of what he was owed. So, this fellow servant did exactly what the official had just done to the gracious king. He begged for mercy from him. He fell down to the ground in submission and cried, "Please, please be patient and I will repay you." Since this amount was much smaller, this payback was actually possible.

Though the official had been shown compassion when he uttered those words, he responded in a completely opposite manner. There was no compassion, no mercy, and absolutely no love. He threw the fellow-servant into prison until this man paid back every denarius he owed. Unfortunately for the official, a group of his own people (fellow-servants to the king) happened to be strolling by. The Lord Jesus described his actions as grieving them terribly, so they all left to report it to the king in detail. They knew that this was unacceptable behavior for someone who had just received so much mercy! When the king discovered what the grievous act his official had committed, the official was summoned.

As this servant stood before him a second time, the king rebuked him and said, "You wicked servant! I forgave all the debt you had because you pleaded with me. Couldn't you have had mercy on your fellow-servant in the same way that I had mercy on you?" Notice this sovereign rebuked the man for not following his example. Then his majesty became angry and commanded that the servant be handed over to the torturers until all of the ten thousand talents had been repaid. Of course, this was impossible, so he would spend his life in prison. The Lord ends the story with a warning, "So will the heavenly Father do to you, if you don't forgive your brother from the heart!" These were stern words.

Here Jesus (the master) was talking to Peter and His other disciples! He is not speaking to unbelievers because God is not their heavenly Father! He may be their creator, but He is not their Father. Rather than interpreting every detail of the parable, which is not necessary, let's get to Jesus' second point. The debt of our sin against God is so great that we could not pay it back in an eternity of punishment or a lifetime of good deeds (the torture until paid back). The sins people commit against us, no matter what they consist of, are very small in comparison to our sins against God (ten thousand talents vs. one hundred). As He demonstrated full and complete forgiveness of our sins, we are to do the same to others (the king felt compassion and released him). If not, we will experience the discipline and training of the Lord, and it will not be pleasant (threw him into prison)! God disciplines His children as a loving Father (Hebrews 12:7-8).

A Modern Anecdote

Due to a large immigration movement, the population of the western world now represents many different cultures and values. As people of different cultures meet, fall in love, marry, and raise children in their new country, often there is a clash of cultural values between the children and parents within the family. Though she did not know it at the time, this was the issue that one such young lady was facing when she came in for counseling.

She explained that she had problems in her relationships with men. As soon as she came near to "falling in love," the young lady would inevitably push the men away. She could accomplish this feat by providing numerous "mixed signals." This would utterly confuse the men so they would give up and end the relationship. Though she thought about it often, she could not figure out the reason for this endless cycle.

After a short time, we discovered that she had unresolved issues with her father. Though this might not always be the case, it was with her. She felt that her father had treated her mother in a demanding and demeaning way, and she did not like it. When I asked for examples, she told me that her father bossed her mother around and expected her mother to obey every command of his. She described her mother as acting like "like a little puppy dog" following him all around the house. He spoke and she listened. Whatever her father wanted, her mother did. This angered her greatly.

When I probed further, she gave more specific details. He would ask her to get him a drink of water, and she would run to get it. Though he could have gotten up and served himself. Also, he wanted dinner on the table as soon as he got home and refused to ever help her in the kitchen. The daughter was appalled. Sometimes, his tone of voice became harsh and unkind. When she left for college, she was so glad to get out of the house and be rid of him once and for all.

Then she ran out of money and had to move home. Now, she was back in this toxic environment. The father's behavior did appear a bit out of sync with western cultural norms, but it was not abusive. I asked her if he had ever mistreated her, and she said, "Never! In fact, he always treated me better than my mom. It made me suspicious that it was all an act. I don't trust men." Why should she? She thought that the most important man in her life had failed her, why would she trust another man? After discovering that her mother and father were immigrants from different cultures, things began to clear up. We took some time to study how the roles of men and women differed in each of their cultures and the western culture she had embraced.

It dawned on her that her father was simply following the cultural values of the country he came from. Though the mother's values were less restrictive than her husband's, she loved him and enjoyed caring for him. She did not mind acting in accordance with his views. It was the daughter that did not like it. She was viewing the situation from a third western cultural perspective. When she was asked if she had ever shared her feelings with her father, she responded, "No! He is evil and wouldn't understand." I explained to her from the Scriptures that God desired her to gently confront him. He certainly deserved the chance to explain his actions at the very least.

Gentle confrontation is not simply to blast a person for his sin, but to see the situation from both sides. She also needed to consider that she may have been wrong in her view of his behavior over these years which led to her intense bitterness toward him. She might well have been angry because she misunderstood her parents' views of their different cultural roles. She would need to repent of this anger and ask for her father's forgiveness. Whatever she decided to do, God would want her to forgive her father just as He had forgiven her for whatever wrongs she had committed in her life.

When she heard this, she stood up and marched out of my office. I heard her mumbling, "I'll never forgive him!" A month later, she gave me a call to let me know that the Holy Spirit had deeply convicted her for the bitterness. The Holy Spirit always convicts of sin and encourages us to act on it.

So, she decided to go to her father and gently confront the man. After an extremely long conversation, she finally began to understand him better. He explained to her how much he loved her and how sorry he was. She told him how sorry she was for harboring such bitterness for so long. This restored the relationship, and they began the process of building it to a new level. This came about because the young woman was willing to gently confront her father. We must do the same.

Chapter 11

Forgive the Forgiven

From practical experience, we know that when Christians have transgressed us, it is not always easy to forgive them. Believers can commit some horrible sins against us that can do great damage to our lives and the lives of those we love. Many people can share stories of believers in a local church who have hurt them. The church has problems because it is made up of people who have problems. The real question is, "How do we handle these problems when they arise?" We are to forgive. Sometimes, this is difficult. When this occurs, one way of resolving this dilemma is to consider all the sins that we have committed against God. God has forgiven so much more. We put away any distinctions in who they are or what they have done to us and forgive. In this chapter, we will learn that not only should we forgive believers because we are forgiven, but also because they are already forgiven by God.

A Typical Scenario

Have you ever had or heard a conversation with a spouse, parent, or friend about another friend that went something like this? You say or hear, "Do you see my magazine? I just loaned it to my friend. His two-year-old son got ahold of it, and now it is destroyed. I was going to pass the magazine to my brother. He loves these things. Every time I have loaned this guy something, it happens again. I am done. I have had enough with him. I am so angry! (Person comments.) What? I don't care if he is a Christian. If he ever comes to me and asks for forgiveness, I'm not forgiving him. And don't quote me any Bible passages. I will never ever forgive him. Do you really understand? Never!"

Here is a perfect example of a believer stuck in bitterness and anger over repeated infractions. How can we overcome such a difficult situation? How can we conquer a powerful unwillingness to show forgiveness to another saint, even if we already know that the Lord desires that we do so? What other truths must we also consider besides the principles we have already learned? Another way is to simply realize that the sins against us that believers commit have already been forgiven by God!

A Scriptural Principle

We must once again begin thinking differently about the person and the transgression to overcome this problem. This brings us to principle eleven which is "we must know that believers who transgress us are already forgiven for their sins." This is an obvious truth, but it is not often considered in this type of circumstance. Whether Christians who have transgressed us have asked for our forgiveness or not, our Holy God and Father has already forgiven them eternally. Whether those who sin against us, as believers, have asked Him for forgiveness or not, the Lord God will handle that relationally. Whether the saints who have sinned against us have asked for forgiveness or not, God will also handle that issue with them as He handles the issue with us.

That is the direct work of His Spirit. We can confront, but He has to work in their hearts. If we have difficulty forgiving another believer, we must consider that those sins against us were nailed to the cross when they received Jesus as Savior and Lord. We may claim all the forgiveness that God gives to us, but we don't always want to think that the Lord has already forgiven the sins they have committed against us through Christ's death on the cross (Colossians 2:13-14).

A Biblical Explanation

Let us study God's forgiveness, not in the light of our own sins, but in the light of deeds against us by other Christians. In the introduction of this book, I mentioned Exodus 34:6-7. In this passage, Moses asked God if he could see His glory. God could only allow him to see the backside, as it were, so He would not be consumed. As God physically manifested Himself to Moses, you may remember that He also verbally declared his glory with these words, "Yahweh passed by before him, and proclaimed, "Yahweh! Yahweh, a merciful and gracious God, slow to anger, and abundant in loving kindness and truth, keeping loving kindness for thousands."

Now, let's read the last part of God's revelation about His character with the wicked deeds of believers against us in our minds. The Lord is "forgiving iniquity and disobedience and sin" of other saints against us. God's glory is manifested when He forgives the sins of others against us. It is a part of God's nature to forgive the sin of other believers against us. His forgiveness extends not only to our sins against others but to others' sins against us. One of the primary reasons we are to forgive is that they are already forgiven by our God. They transgressed against Him first. Yet, God had enough grace, mercy, and love to forgive them and so should we.

In Luke 17:3-4, Jesus teaches, "Be careful. If your brother sins against you, rebuke him. If he repents, forgive him." He commands forgiveness of others again. Then the Lord Jesus exhorts, "If he sins against you seven times in the day, and seven times returns, saying, 'I repent,' you shall forgive him." Why should we? One reason is that God, our Father, has

113

already forgiven them. In Matthew 26:28, at the last supper, Jesus declared, "For this is My blood of the covenant, which is poured out for many for forgiveness of sins." The blood of Christ was not simply poured out for us and the sins we commit against others but also poured out for others and the sins they commit against us. What an amazing change in perspective. So, when I consider the sins of a spouse, parent, child, friend, fellow student, co-worker, or neighbor against me and do not want to forgive, I must remember that if they are a believer God has already forgiven him or her.

In Ephesians 1:7, Paul says, "In Him we have redemption through His blood." That redemption extends to the sins of other Christians against us. Then he adds, "The forgiveness of our trespasses, according to the riches of His grace." The forgiveness according to the riches of God's grace not only extends to our trespasses but those who trespass against us. In Hebrews 9:22, the author describes the impact of Christ's death in these words, "Without shedding of blood there is no forgiveness." The shedding of Jesus Christ's blood on that cursed cross providing forgiveness for all our sins, provided forgiveness for all those saints who have sinned against us.

In 1 John 1:7, the beloved disciple John declares, "But if we walk in the light, as he is in the light, we have fellowship with one another, and the blood of Jesus Christ, his Son, cleanses us from all sin." The blood cleanses "us" from all our sins even against each other. Then he continues in 1 John 2:12, "I write to you, little children, because your sins are forgiven you for His Name's sake." The biblical expression "for His Name's sake" carries the idea of "all that He is and has done." The name of a person represented all of whom the person was and did. The sins that believers commit against us have been forgiven in the name of and for the sake of the Lord Jesus Christ who died on the cross for their sins as well as ours.

Paul was the Lord's classic example in 1 Timothy 1:15-17. The Christians who had loved ones injured or killed because of the apostle had to accept him into the church. They had to forgive his atrocities against them and the ones they loved the most. That must have been tough. As we can so clearly see, all of these passages include our forgiveness when we sin against others. We love to rejoice in this truth. Here is another equally important truth: these verses also include the forgiveness of others when they transgress us!

In fact, here is a beautiful pattern: we are being forgiven for our sins against the brethren as they are being forgiven for their sins against us. This is utterly forgiveness upon forgiveness. Often, we get stuck and do not want to forgive our brothers and sisters in Christ. Yet, we so desperately want God to forgive our sins against them. We cannot have it both ways. If we are to receive God's forgiveness, so are they! May this truth assist us in forgiving others.

An Ancient Portrait

Let's now take a second look at the story of the Prodigal Son. This tale can also be viewed from the perspective of the older brother to gain some insight into why Christians do not forgive their brothers and sisters in the light of the last two principles mentioned. In Luke 15, the older brother was unwilling to forgive his younger brother even though the younger brother had repented. We will pick up the story after the prodigal son returns and the father throws a great banquet to celebrate his return.

The older brother arrived at the house after a day's work in the field managing the estate. He heard loud music and dancing which meant people were celebrating something inside his home. There were no servants around. The outside of the estate was empty. All of them were serving the guests. He was standing there completely alone wondering what in the world was going on. He called over one of the boys who were playing outside, since the adults were celebrating, to find out what was happening. He was the eldest son and should have been presiding over any celebration. He had been reduced to someone asking children what was going on. They explained that his youngest brother had come back, and his father had killed a fattened calf. I am sure he thought to himself in utter disbelief, "What? That is impossible? That no good brother of mine is getting the greatest celebration a family can have? What about me? I have been faithful to my father all along. I have nothing!"

Then the boys explained further. His father had received his younger brother back safe and sound. The Greek words utilized actually emphasize the father's response to his son's return. The son had been received back in peace and with full restoration. This made the older brother very angry! So, the son absolutely refused to go into his own home! When dad found out, he came running out. What a great, warm, and loving father he was! He would not let the older son stay outside and wallow in his own anger, bitterness, and stubbornness. He pursued the older son in his sin as he did the younger in his. In his love, grace, and mercy, the father pleaded with the older son to come inside and celebrate the return of his dear younger brother. They were all a family again!

The older son could only think about himself. Instead, He rebuked his merciful father and described how he himself had served his father many years. He had never disobeyed him. The older son had never even been given a young goat, so he could celebrate with his own friends. This response is loaded with meaning. He turned this all around and made it all about him. Why was his father not concerned about his feelings? He had continually served and obeyed him. In his description, the older son had reduced his relationship with his father to nothing more than servitude and obedience. He ignored the return of his brother and did not even appeal to the father's love for him. Why didn't he say, "Father, we love each other, why haven't you given me a celebration?" Why not even an appeal to love, however weak it would have been? Why? There was no relationship there in the first place. Notice, he tells his father that he has never even had a celebration with his friends, not his family. His buddies were all that mattered to him. It was not his father or brother.

What a blow to the father! Neither of the two was worth anything to him. Then the older brother lets us in on a little secret. He was keeping tabs on his younger brother all along. He revealed the prostitution his little brother had indulged in and then asked his father why he would give his brother a celebration with a fattened calf. He threw his little brother's squandering of the father's goods into his face and still he was restored. The older son tried to rile his father up and turn his warm heart from compassion to bitterness. There was nothing but accusations.

Not once, did the older son ask how his brother was or even if he had repented. The father did not even explain himself. The father simply told him that he had always been with him, and all of his property was his. Then he explained that his little brother had been dead and was now alive; that is, his younger brother was dead to the family and was back. He was lost but now was found. The son was concentrating on the loss of their possessions and property, but his father was focusing on the restoration of their relationships and the rebuilding of their family.

Jesus told this story to point out that the Pharisees (older brother) had hard hearts toward God, our Father. They were concerned only about righteous works and outward religion, pomp, and circumstance. God is concerned about repentance and His gracious forgiveness. They did not truly have an inward, spiritual relationship with God but only an outward temporal relationship. For our purposes, let us focus on the older brother who refused to even consider the possibility of ever forgiving his younger brother.

First, he was unwilling to forgive because he had never himself asked his father for forgiveness. Why? He thought he had never done anything wrong. He told the father he had never disobeyed him or ever failed to serve him. That is impossible. Since the older son had never gone to his father and begged for mercy, how could he in anyway understand how his father could show mercy to his brother? When we are not continually going before God with our sins begging for his mercy, then it is harder to show mercy to others. How can we forgive when forgiven, if we think we do not need forgiveness? Those believers who think they are always right and have all of the answers have a tremendous difficulty forgiving the other person in a relationship. If this occurs, God will discipline that person to fully understand what a sinner he or she is.

Second, he would not recognize that his father who was the foremost person transgressed had already forgiven him. The primary person in that family was the father, if he could ultimately forgive then so could the other family members. The main person transgressed in a sin against us is God. If He can forgive them, so ought we. When a brother or sister transgresses us, we need to acknowledge that our Father has already forgiven that very transgression on the cross of Jesus Christ. We must view the situation from the perspective of God, not from our perspective. The older brother refused to view the situation from his father's perspective so he would not forgive him.

Third, the older son was looking only at what he had lost. He was focusing on the transgression. He kept churning the sins against him over and over. When his little brother had repented, he could not see past the sins to see what would be gained. He would gain his little brother back. This is what the father saw. He looked past the material to the relational. We must look far past the temporal and toward the spiritual. Since God has forgiven them already, we must also forgive.

A Modern Anecdote

One of my counselees grew up with a mother who had a serious alcohol problem. Since his father had passed away when he was about six, his mother did not take it very well. Alcohol was her drug of choice whenever, which was often, she felt overwhelmed by the kids (six of them), her job, the bills, and loneliness. Many times, after a drinking bout, his mother would arrive home and leave their front door wide open. When he awoke to use the restroom, he would see the front door open and think someone was breaking into the house. Other times, she would forget to buy food, and the kids would have to take whatever was in the house and turn it into school lunches. Sometimes, this meant a large piece of cheese or a small cereal box.

There were several incidences where his mother would fall and injure herself, and he would bandage her up. Then, he would fall asleep fearing she would bleed to death during the night. As he got older, the problem just worsened. Often, she would fall asleep on the couch with a lit cigarette in her hand. He would take turns with his other siblings to stay up late and watch her until she had fallen asleep drunk. Then, he would quietly take the cigarette and put it out to prevent the house from burning down. She spent much of the small amount of money they had on liquor and could not pay the bills. When bill collectors came around, they (the children present at the time) would hide behind the couch. This way the person would think no one was home. When he would talk to her about many of these events, she would respond with a long diatribe about the woes of a single parent who was doing the best that she possibly could. At nineteen, the mother finally entered a rehab program and sobered up.

After he had grown up and had his own family, he visited his mother on either Thanksgiving or Christmas every year. Besides this time, he never called her or invited her to any of his children's events and activities. When his last child was close to graduating from college, she casually said to him, "How come you never invited me to any of my grandkid's functions when they were growing up?" This startled him. He could not respond because he did have an answer. For several months, he pondered that question, "Why hadn't he invited her to his children's activities?" He had spent every summer traveling to see his siblings but never his mother.

One day it dawned on him that he had completely walled her off from his heart. He had not invited her because there was no real relationship. He had no feelings for his mother. In fact, he was angry and bitter and had never forgiven her for what she had done. He had punished her unknowingly by not allowing her into his life or the lives of his children. Then, he decided that she deserved it, and that was that.

A year later, the woman received Jesus Christ as Savior and Lord. In the first year of her salvation, his sister gently confronted His mother concerning all of the problems that she had caused in their growing up years. She told her that she deeply regretted what happened and asked his sister for forgiveness. He decided if she called to reconcile, he would refuse to speak to her or even see her. The pain was far too deep, and the scares were too numerous.

What could he do to break this anger and bitterness that had a death grip upon him before his mother called, so he could forgive her? I explained to him all that we have just studied in this chapter. First, he should compare the sins his mother had committed against him with the sins he had committed against God. God had forgiven Him and desired him to forgive His mother. Secondly, he must recognize that she had sinned against God first as she was sinning against him. God had already forgiven her for what she had done to him on the cross of His Beloved Son. He needed to ask the Holy Spirit to help him grasp these important truths so he could fully forgive her. After much prayer over several days, he was able to open his mind and heart to these truths and forgive her for the sins she had committed against him, as His Lord had already done on the cross.

Chapter 12

Forgive the Lost

When people have transgressed us, sometimes it becomes difficult to forgive them. It may take some time. People can do some hurtful and destructive things to us, and we might get stuck in bitterness because we are unwilling to forgive. A way we can get "unstuck" is to consider all the sins we have committed against God. Once we realize that Jesus made no distinctions in forgiving us when we received His Son, it will be easier to make no distinctions ourselves. Why? God did not refuse to forgive us because of who we were or because of the gravity or extent of our sins. So, we are to do the same to others.

If those who transgressed us are believers also and we are struggling with forgiveness, here is another approach. We must consider this truth: whatever they may have done to us has already been forgiven on the cross. How can we not forgive what God has already forgiven? Regarding those who are unbelievers, we must view them much differently to get unstuck from bitterness. Rather than considering them as just wicked people who deserve punishment, we should see them as lost and desperately in need of salvation. This will be the topic of discussion in this chapter.

A Typical Scenario

Have you ever had or heard of someone looking out the window of his home and having the following conversation with his wife? He says, "Honey, you've got to come and see this! Do you remember that young guy down the street who we shared the gospel with the other day? The neighbor three doors down? The guy that told us he wasn't interested. He has two large garbage bags filled with glass bottles tied to his bike and ran into our car. The bags just broke right in front of our driveway. I can't believe this! Now, there's glass all over the street and a dent in the car. He's trying to pick up the pieces with his bare hands. Those pieces are way too small! Is he crazy? What a fool! Oh, he's going to pay, all right! There will be no forgiveness here! Honey!? What are you doing? Where are you going with that broom?"

This man had been caught in the act of being shamed by his forgiving wife. All he could think about was himself. His wife thought about the neighbor. The man saw his neighbor as a wicked man in need of judgment, and his wife saw him as lost in need of salvation. She ran out to demonstrate the love and compassion of Christ. The husband did not want to forgive him, but his gracious wife already had! This attitude sometimes takes ahold of us. Unbelievers hurt us in some way, and we do not want to forgive them. Then someone like this wife is able to. How does that happen? How could she show such forgiveness and we struggle with it? It simply has to do with perspective. She saw him as lost, not wicked.

A Scriptural Principle

Now we come to the next principle. The twelfth principle is "we must view unbelievers as lost to forgive." This means we should view those who transgress us with the eyes and heart of God. In order to forgive unbelievers for hurting us, we must first see them differently. We must have the divine perspective of our Father in heaven. At this time in salvation history, God sees all unbelievers as lost and seeks to save them in His compassion. On the Day of Judgment, God will see them as wicked and seek to punish them in His wrath.

A Biblical Explanation

We know people should be forgiven for everything they have done against us. The Lord Jesus makes no distinction in their beliefs or relationship to Him. With unbelievers, this is sometimes easier said than done. Sometimes, we Christians may get stuck in bitterness and be unwilling to forgive. To overcome this difficulty, Christians must begin to think differently about those who do not know Jesus. When an unbeliever is viewed as a wicked, evil sinner, then it is easy to be bitter and angry. It is simple to curse them into the fire of hell without mercy. This is what happened with James and John, two of the twelve disciples of Jesus.

In Luke 9:51-56, the Lord was on His way to Jerusalem for the final Passover and His ultimate death. He sent some of His disciples into a Samaritan village to obtain lodging. The citizens of the city refused. They hated the Jews, and their feasts and Jesus was a Jew on His way to a feast. As far as they were concerned, this Rabbi was not staying the night in their town. When James and John heard of it, they asked the Lord if they could command fire from heaven to consume the town. The disciples were upset and desired judgment on these unrighteous people. Jesus rebuked them explaining that "He had not come to destroy men's lives, but to save them." When Christ came the first time to earth, He came to save the lost. The second time, He will arrive to judge the wicked. The first time, He views them as lost and desires to save them. The second time, He will have given them all the time they needed to repent, and they did not. Then, He will focus on them as wicked and desire to judge them.

In Luke 19:10, the Lord declared His desire, "For the Son of Man came to seek and to save that which was lost." Jesus spoke of unbelievers, especially Israel, as lost sheep, a lost coin, and a lost son. He viewed unbelievers as lost. We are to view them similarly. We might be in various relationships with unbelievers. At times, they may sin against us. When this happens, to help us in the forgiveness process, we must see them as lost. What does it mean to say the unsaved are lost? When someone is lost, they do not know where they are or where they are going. They cannot find their way. In 1 John 2:11, John paints a picture of the lost as walking in the darkness, not knowing where they are going because the darkness has blinded their eyes. They are stumbling around in the darkness of their own sin and wickedness and the lies and falsehoods of the Devil.

So, if we have a relationship with an unbeliever, why do we expect them to constantly behave like us? Why don't we anticipate them to act lost? Often times, our expectations are too high which makes us even more bitter and angry. You may say, "Aren't they also responsible for their actions?" Of course they are. If they do not come to Christ, they will be judged for every single unkind word or action they commit toward us. They desperately need Christ. Don't they? We could constantly condemn these people as truly wicked and wallow in our anger and bitterness. Or we can share Christ with them and continue in prayer for them. This does not excuse any of their actions toward us, nor the consequences for them. It does not mean they may treat us poorly. This simply has to do with our heart's forgiveness of them.

In Luke 23:34, the Lord Jesus was hanging on the cross, dripping with blood from the crown of thorns and the nails in his hands and feet. In His pain and humiliation, as He was slowly dying, He cried to His Father. For what? He asked Him to forgive His persecutors because they did not know what they were doing. He saw all of these people in the light of their lostness. They were dead, hard, calloused, and blind, but, most of all, ignorant. The Romans, who were doing the dirty work the Jews could not do, did not realize that they were crucifying the King of Kings. The crowd of Jews who were standing around the cross-throwing insults and curses at Him did not understand this was their own Messiah. The frightened disciples, who had hidden from the mob, did not fully comprehend that as His death was at hand, so was His forgiveness of all on the cross. From His death would come the resurrection to a new life in Him. Even many of these rulers, who were caught up in their religious self-righteous pride, did not perceive that a new covenant in His blood had come. They did not see that a new and final priest was now making a final sacrifice for the sins of all men.

In the midst of this horrible chaos, Christ knowing all of this, looked down at their lostness and cried out for the Father's forgiveness. This obviously implies the Lord's own forgiveness in His humanity. Christians know through their understanding of the Scriptures that this prayer could only be fulfilled if all of these lost people received the soon to be risen Son of God as Savior and Lord. Yet, implied in the merciful cry to His Holy Father, is a God who became truly man, and as a man forgave His persecutors, tormentors, and scoffers. How could He do that? How could He keep from becoming bitter and angry, refusing to forgive? He saw them as lost!

An Ancient Portrait

This is what happened when Jonah viewed the people of Nineveh. In the book of Jonah, God had told him to go and preach to them; instead, he was repulsed and fled. He did not want them to be forgiven. They deserved judgment and he was going to make sure they got it. Why? These people were terribly wicked. Yet, the Lord saw them as lost and desired to give them grace. Then God commanded Jonah to travel to the city of Nineveh and preach against the city. So,

Jonah boarded a ship at Joppa that was headed for Tarshish. This city was about as far away from Nineveh as one could get at the time. I am sure that Jonah had hoped God would give up on him since he was too far away.

While on his sea voyage, the Lord sent a great storm. This put the ship on the verge of breaking apart. The ship's crew started throwing the cargo overboard to lighten the ship's load. Then they cried out to their gods for help. While all this commotion was happening, where was the prophet? Jonah was asleep below in the cargo area. How could Jonah be fast asleep? Why wasn't he afraid? Most likely, the prophet knew God may punish him, and frankly he did not care. He would rather die than go to that evil city! Though he was calm in his resolve, the captain of the ship was not. The captain came down and screamed at him. He told him to wake up and call on his God to save them. He refused to do it. Then they cast lots to see which crew member or passenger had caused this storm? The lot fell on Jonah. They demanded him to explain who he was and what he had done. Can you imagine the tension in the crew as they stood there with this stranger that was causing all this havoc?

Jonah declared that he was a Hebrew who feared the God of heaven and earth. He immediately explained that he was a believer in the true God. Then he told them he was on the run from God because he didn't want to obey His command. They must have known right then that this man was special. He wasn't any ordinary Jew, and he wasn't disobeying any ordinary command. Something was seriously wrong. Then, they begged him to explain what the crew could do to calm the storm. I am sure they expected him to repent and offer something to "his god." This was a storm that was about to destroy them all. Even they knew this should be done. Jonah probably startled them by his calm and almost ridiculous response. He told them to throw him overboard. It was his fault and he needed to go. Why didn't Jonah simply repent? God would have calmed the sea, and he could have shared the gospel with this backdrop of God's power and grace.

The prophet could only think about those dirty, wicked, evil Ninevites. Nothing else mattered. The Ninevites were not going to be forgiven if he could help it, even if it cost him his life. Though unbelievers, the crew did not have the heart to follow his advice and throw him overboard. Instead, they tried furiously to row the boat to shore. This was a vain and useless attempt, but they could not kill him. The storm only got worse! So, they begged the Lord God not to hold what they were about to do against them and threw Jonah into the sea. Immediately the storm ceased. Now Jonah was flailing and thrashing in his own stubbornness in the ocean all alone. God could have left him there to die, but that is not His way.

He showed Jonah the forgiveness Jonah did not want the Ninevites to receive. God sent a great fish to swallow him. He was in the stomach of that fish for three days and three nights. While trapped there, Jonah began to reflect on what just happened. He remembered that he been in the depths of the ocean, the currents had engulfed him, and the waves of the ocean were passing over him. At the same time, the weeds had wrapped around his head, and he had come to the edge of life and death. In that moment, he had felt far from the presence of the Lord. He knew he was exactly where he had desired to be. He was away from the Lord. Unfortunately, it was not what he had expected. It never is. As he was about to lose all consciousness, he turned back to God and cried out with a desperate prayer for mercy.

He was literally lost in his own sin and stubbornness. Haven't we all been there before? He desperately needed some compassion from God, and Jonah was begging for His forgiveness. Though these Ninevites were lost also in their stubbornness and sin, Jonah hadn't thought that they might deserve either. Perhaps, the time had come to rethink this obvious contradiction. After having been swallowed up in the depths of the sea by a huge creature, he remained in its belly for three days and nights. It was here that Jonah began to ponder these amazing things. Then, he repented and thanked God for his gracious rescue.

When Jonah had finally submitted to the Lord God and decided to obey Him, God commanded the fish to vomit Jonah onto the shore. It was time to go to Nineveh. Again, the Lord issued His command to Jonah: preach to the city of Nineveh. These Ninevites were lost, and God wanted them found. So, Jonah arose and went to the city. Then, he walked from one end of it to the other proclaiming God's merciful message. He declared that they were to repent of their evil deeds or be destroyed in forty days.

This city was the capitol of Assyria which was the most powerful nation on earth. Who could overthrow them with such power? Humanly speaking, no individual or nation could, but Jonah was speaking for the Lord. His God can do anything He desires. His God meant business. When the King of Nineveh heard Jonah's message, he arose from his royal throne, threw off his royal robe, covered himself in sackcloth and ashes, and issued a proclamation in the land.

The king commanded that all people and animals put on sackcloth and ashes and fast out of sorrow and repentance for their wicked and violent ways. They should then pray that Jonah's God would have mercy on them and withdraw His burning anger and wrath of judgment upon them. The one hundred and twenty thousand people of the city obeyed from the greatest to the least with sincerity. So, God stopped the calamity that was about to come upon the Ninevites and and showed them mercy.

Sometimes, like Jonah we view the unsaved as only evil and wicked. When they commit a transgression against us, we do not want to forgive them, nor do we desire them to come to Christ. Let them die in their sins! Our Father is not like this. He has tremendous compassion for them as He had for us. Must we forgive the evil, especially when it hurts us? How about when it hurt God's only righteous, beloved, holy Son? This is a total game changer in perspective toward all who are unbelievers. It changed Jonah's perspective, and now it must also change our perspective. God desires for us to see them as He sees them. The unsaved are lost and walk in darkness. All unbelievers do not spiritually know their right hand from their left. They should be forgiven.

A Modern Anecdote

Problems with fathers date back a long time. Every family has had one or more male family members who choose not to fulfill their responsibilities as fathers. They discovered it was quite easy to have children but extremely difficult to care for them. For the children, this often leads to issues in later life. One such child, now a man, came in for counseling. As he entered my counseling office, I was introduced to an upbeat, happy, and seemingly fulfilled man who didn't seem to have a care in the world. He was successful and happily married. His children were all grown up, educated, happily married, and successful also. He had become a believer in his twenties and desired to love the Lord with all his heart and obey him. His wife and children were believers, and his first grandson had just received the Lord Jesus Christ.

After our first session, I discovered that all was not what it seemed. He had glaring issues in his life which were under the surface, unseen by others, including his own family. He felt inadequate as a husband, uncomfortable as a father, and inferior as a man. He was so tired of these feelings but could not rid himself of them. No amount of prayer or bible study could solve this problem, and he did not know why. When feelings come up without present circumstances warranting them, then it's time to look into the past. During several sessions, we discovered that he had some real issues with his father.

His father was a heavy drinker and could be violent with anyone who disagreed with him when he was in this state. When the son was seven years old, his parents divorced over it. Then, his father moved out. As alcohol took over his father's life, he almost never visited his son. As a result, his son never learned the mechanical skills that he possessed, received any advice on the childhood or adolescent issues he faced, only saw his father shouting at his mother when they had to interact, and eventually forgot any relationship they had had before the divorce. In his son's mind, he was always a dark shadow which was lurking in the background never showing himself.

Sometime after the son had graduated from college, the father finally sobered up. The son thought perhaps now he would come around, but to his disappointment he did not. Suddenly, he passed away. The son refused to go to his funeral and mourn him. In fact, deep down the son was glad that he was now gone. As we spoke about his father, the son became angrier and angrier, until he burst into tears.

He suddenly realized he was full of bitterness for this man who was supposed to be his father, and he was now dead. The anger and bitterness began to pour out of him like dark, murky water. He quickly became aware that he blamed his father for his feelings. His father had not been the example necessary for him to learn how to be a husband. It made him always feel inadequate.

His father had not demonstrated how to be a parent to his children. As a result, he always felt like he could be a better father when he was actually a great "dad." His father had not taught him the mechanical skills that he so desperately needed to even fix the simplest of problems with his house or car. This made him feel like less of a man. He had not realized that every time one of these feelings occurred, he blamed his father. He felt like his father had robbed him of his needed preparation for manhood which led to his inability to experience the full joy of being with his family. This could not be recompensed. He could never have these precious years back.

I told him that he was completely justified in his feelings. It was the father's responsibility to fulfill his role in his son's preparation for his adult life, and his father had completely failed him. Now, he was gone and could never reconcile the relationship, but he still needed to forgive his father. Once this was done by faith, then the feelings would slowly fade away. When I discovered that his father was an unbeliever, I shared the principles in this chapter with him and we read the story of Jonah aloud. As we read that story, I could hear him quietly mumbling and muttering to himself. The Holy Spirit began opening his eyes to see that he was facing the same issues as Jonah. At the end, he announced, "I know what I have to do, please go with me." Several days later, we drove to his father's gravesite, and the man confronted his dead father and then forgave him. He had understood how lost his father truly was and how desperately he needed to be found.

Chapter 13

Keep No Records

If we have a broken relationship with our spouse, partner, boyfriend, girlfriend, child, parent, friend, neighbor, fellow student, or co-worker, or even an acquaintance, we learned the Lord God desires that we go to him or her and reconcile the relationship through forgiveness. This includes what we do with past sins. The next step concerns any mental records we may want to keep.

A Typical Scenario

Have you ever had or heard a conversation with a spouse that went something like this? You say, "Wow! I have been waiting for this coffee all morning. (Sip coffee). Yuck! No cream. Honey! Did you remember to purchase the cream? (Person responds in the negative.) No! Why not? I gave you one thing to do and once again you forgot. This is the third time in a month you forgot the cream for my coffee. Last week, you forgot my shirts at the cleaners. The week before that, you also forgot to pick up the kids at school. I cannot depend on you for anything. (Talk to yourself.) The next time she needs me to do something, I'm going to forget! Let's see how she likes that! That'll teach her!" Notice, the spouse mentions the past mistakes over and over. Why do we keep bringing up the past? Why do we keep tabs on people who have hurt us? Why must we continue to punish our spouses, children, parents, friends, co-workers, or even neighbors who may have offended us again and again? It discourages them, can devastate them, punish them over and over, or make them angry and bitter. No good comes of it.

135

A Scriptural Principle

Once forgiveness comes, we must take the next important step. The thirteenth principle is "we must not keep records of the sins against us." Simply, we must forgive and forget. Obviously, we cannot actually forget, but we are to treat past offenses as if the transgressions are over, finished, and done with. When Paul describes Christian love in 1 Corinthians 13:5, he uses these very words to characterize it. He declares that love "takes no account of evil." This English phrase is two words in the Greek which mean "makes no record of it" or "no longer takes it into account." It was a banking term in the ancient world speaking of keeping a record of deposits and withdrawals in an account. It means keeping a record of someone's wrong.

Paul is indicating that love does not keep records. People do not demonstrate true love by keeping a record in their minds and memories of others' transgressions against them for the purpose of punishing them. Through forgiveness, the transgressions are forgotten and permanently removed from the ledger of our minds. This is a supernatural, divine act. Our memories of hurtful words or actions of a loved one may be triggered by a movie, book, song, or event, yet we make that memory of no account. It comes back up into the ledger of our minds, and through a conscious effort, we erase it once again. Every time it surfaces, we erase it. This is what God does for us.

A Biblical Explanation

This constant record keeping begins in the mind, not from the mouth. Our minds indulge in the continual rehearsing of what others have done to us, and this produces much anger and bitterness. These negative feelings bring forth strife and conflict as they transform themselves into harsh words and actions. Centuries ago, Solomon described this very process in Proverbs 30:33 when he penned, "For as the churning of milk produces butter, and the wringing of the nose produces blood; so, the forcing [churning] of wrath produces strife." A barrage of our transgressions is thrown at us or vice versa which destroys and demolishes our relationships. Why? This cannon fire leads to fighting, arguing, and quarreling which never builds and renews relationships, only crushes them.

In Proverbs 10:12, the king asserts, "Hatred stirs up strife, but love covers all wrongs." Real love does not write wrongs down upon the heart in order to use it against someone later; it covers over all of them. The recording of transgressions in our minds and repeating them in our words causes hatred of the offenders leading to disputes, clashes, and altercations. In Proverbs 17:9, he continues, "He who covers an offense promotes love; but he who repeats a matter separates best friends." Here Solomon is speaking of (covering over) not revealing the offense of one friend against another. This will promote love between them. When the offense is revealed, the one offended separates from the offender.

This also describes what happens in a relationship when people keep bringing up (revealing) the past offenses over and over again, never "covering it over" in love. Suddenly, they find themselves utterly alone. In 1 Peter 4:8, the apostle reiterates this same important principle when he exhorts his readers, "And above all things be earnest in your love among yourselves, for love covers a multitude of sins." Notice, Peter describes an effort that is earnest in our love for one another. This covering over in love requires an earnest effort to really love someone. It is so easy to keep bringing things up to others who have wronged us rather than just holding our tongues. It is difficult and requires much effort to keep silent in our love and forgiveness.

This lack of record-keeping does not have to do with the consequences and necessary restitution one may require for the transgression. This does not in any way mean that the transgressor has a free ticket to do whatever they want and then say, "Sorry, you have to forgive and forget." This does not at all mean that we should never alter our behavior or set up boundaries in our relationships when sin continues to happen over and over. Instead, this lack of record-keeping involves the response of forgiveness itself.

Once our sins have been forgiven, we should not have the transgressions brought up over and over again, so we have to relive them or perhaps experience the consequences again and again. When this happens, it usually will produce anger or a sorrow that will lead to real despair in the relationship. It will make us feel as if we will be held accountable for what we did the remainder of time we partake in the relationship. How can someone live in a relationship with another who says, "I may never get over this!" The reverse will also be true. We cannot put others through this torment and torture.

When Paul visited Corinth, someone had opposed him vehemently to his face. He had questioned Paul's motives and actions in ministry. After the church had disciplined this instigator, the man repented. Then Paul was very concerned about the man's restoration back into the fellowship. In 2 Corinthians 2:7, he admonished the church to "forgive him and comfort him, lest by any means such a one should be swallowed up with his excessive sorrow." The apostle was worried that after this one who opposed him had repented, the church would not fully accept him back. He did not want the church to shun him or avoid him. The saints were not to bring up his past actions against Paul because this would only lead to the man's excessive sorrow. If we keep bringing up the same offense, this could lead to the transgressor being swallowed up in sorrow or despair.

This principle of forgiving and forgetting comes right out of the character of our merciful and compassionate God. Once people have received Jesus as their Lord and Savior, their sins are not only forgiven but forgotten. In Isaiah 43:25, God describes this process in the following words, "I, even I, am he who blots out your transgressions for my own sake; and I will not remember your sins."

In Jeremiah 31:34, the Lord again proclaims, "And they shall teach no more every man his neighbor, and every man his brother, saying,' Know Yahweh; for they shall all know me, from their least to their greatest, says Yahweh: for I will forgive their iniquity, and their sin will I remember no more." In Hebrews 8:12, God announces, "For I will be merciful to their unrighteousness. I will remember their sins and lawless deeds no more." Now, it is not that the Lord does not actually remember; instead, He renders it of no account. It is over and done. It will never be brought up again. So, when someone hurts us, we need to act like our God does toward us. We need to forgive them and forget the offense by rendering those offenses as of no account in our minds. They won't be brought up again.

An Ancient Portrait

The best example of someone who did not keep records is Jesus Christ Himself. When the Lord encountered Martha and Mary a second time on the way to raising their brother from the dead, He didn't bring up the past mistakes Martha had made. You may remember the first story of Martha and Mary in Luke 10:38-41. Mary was seated at the feet of Jesus listening to Him teach, while her sister Martha was in the kitchen making preparations. She became so overwhelmed that she stormed into the presence of Jesus and demanded that He command Mary to help her. Patiently, Jesus refused and explained to Martha that Mary had chosen the better part which was teaching over service. Mary was seen later at the house of Simon the leper anointing Jesus with oil in worship and adoration.

Their next recorded encounter together is found in John chapter eleven. It begins after the public ministry of Jesus had ended. Lazarus, Martha and Mary's brother, was very ill and deteriorating rapidly. The Lord received a message from Martha and Mary saying, "Lord, the one whom you love is sick." Jesus loved all three of them and they knew each other well. They believed He was the Savior. They knew He had healed so many people in Palestine, many of whom He did not know. Now, their brother, whom He loved, was sick.

After receiving the message, Jesus casually remarked to His disciples that the sickness of His dear friend wasn't for the purpose of bringing on death but for the purpose of demonstrating the glory of God. This was information only Jesus as God could know. He knew the world was about to see something so dramatic that people would speak of it for many years. To present His great glory to the world, Lazarus unfortunately would have to die for a short time, so Jesus stayed two more days. Though the Lord loved Martha and Mary, they would now have to endure one of man's most difficult experiences, the death of a family member.

By the time Jesus arrived, Lazarus had been in the tomb four days. A crowd of people had gathered around Martha and Mary attempting to console them. When Martha heard that Jesus had finally arrived, she came running, and she wasn't planning on their reunion being pleasant. Martha stood before the Lord and questioned Him as to why He did not arrive earlier and save her brother! She then implied that he could still raise Him from the dead if He so desired, since God always answered His prayers.

Before I mention what Jesus said to her, I want to take a moment to mention what He did not say. Jesus did not say, "Well, here we go again, Martha. The last time we saw each other you complained about Mary and her unwillingness to help you in the kitchen. This time, you are complaining that I did not come quick enough to save your brother. We are done. I have had enough! Let Lazarus rot in the grave for all I care." He did not respond in this way because He was not keeping a record of all her wrongs.

Instead, the Lord had forgiven her other transgression and was not going to bring it up again. This is critical to building strong relationships and is a good example of the principle we are studying. He did not allow what happened in the past to get in the way of the present. Instead, Jesus explained to Martha that Lazarus will rise again. Martha responded that she knew he would be resurrected on the last day and affirmed her faith in Him. He did not say he was going to raise her brother. After their time together, he asked for Mary.

I am sure that she left disappointed. She then went and sent Mary to Jesus secretly because Jesus wanted to see her. Perhaps, she thought Mary could talk some sense into Him, so He would raise their brother from the dead. They wanted him back! That is all they could think about. When Mary saw Jesus, she fell at His feet and questioned Him in the exact manner that Martha had done. Once again, if Jesus had come when they called, Lazarus would still be alive today. They had seen His power, they knew He could heal him, but He didn't. Notice, Jesus does not rebuke her for her temporal blindness (not seeing his death in the light of heaven).

Then, Jesus traveled with the sisters and the crowds of people to the cave where the brother had been buried. When he arrived, Jesus commanded them to move away the stone that was covering the entrance to the brother's tomb. Martha once again interjected. She commented that there would be a great stench because he had been in the tomb four days. This implied that the Lord Jesus simply wanted to see the body and perhaps say goodbye. Again, Jesus doesn't bring the record up and blast her for this third infraction. Instead, He simply reminded her that He said if she believed in Him, she would see His glory. Of course, she thought it would be on the last day not a few moments later. Since Lazarus had been in the grave for so long, all would know that what they saw was not a magician's trick. Jesus could raise even the dead!

When they removed the stone, Jesus thanked the Father and then commanded loudly, "Lazarus, come out!" Can you imagine the hush among the people? What? Did He just say what they thought He said? Just as suddenly, the dead man came hobbling out still being bound hand and foot by the wrappings that encompassed him. Jesus told them to free him, and let the man go. Nothing was said about Martha or Mary's indiscretion before the Lord. The Lord had forgiven them and did not keep records. Many believed in Him. So, when people sin against us, we are to forgive and not keep mental records of the offenses. This frees us from the torment of churning it over and over and keeps them from excessive sorrow or despair in the relationship. We are to forgive and forget. Remember, this does not refer to the need for setting boundaries, providing consequences, or expecting restitution. We cannot go over and over what someone has done against us.

A Modern Anecdote

A teenage daughter stomped angrily into my office with her mother in tow and demanded, "I want to go first." She explained that as far back as she could remember her mother took detailed mental notes on every "bad thing" (her words) she had done. If the daughter repeated even one of these, out of her mother's mouth would come a long list of infractions she had committed. It overwhelmed her and made her feel really stupid. She admitted that she was a bit clumsy and didn't always pay attention to what she was doing. I asked if she could give me several concrete examples. At seven, she was playing the game of Hide and Seek in the living room and knocked over a lamp which put a small chip at the base. She was reprimanded and spent the evening in her room. She told her mother how sorry she was. Then the daughter promised her mother that the next time she would be much more careful.

Two years later, the daughter was removing a box of her princess dolls out of the top of the closet, lost her balance, and the box came tumbling to the ground spilling out all the dolls. One of the dolls took flight and hit a figurine that her mother had purchased for her on a trip and broke its finger off. When her mother heard the commotion, she stormed into the room, saw the broken figurine, and then screamed, "Okay, that's twice now. What is wrong with you?" After a detailed description of what she had done to the lamp, the mother marched her down the stairs and pointed to the chip. The young lady had felt so upset that she ran to her room, shut the door, and sobbed. The mother shouted through the door, "You are grounded for three days young lady! Once that figurine is repaired, it will be put away. That way you cannot destroy it." This only made things even worse for the young girl as she wept and wept in her room.

At twelve, she made herself a snack and went to watch television in the family room. Her mom had told her many times to be careful with any food she brought in. The carpet was new. She decided to watch a scary movie and eat some nachos. In the movie, a monster jumped out from behind a corner and startled her to such an extent that she threw the plate up into the air. As the nachos, cheese, and salsa landed on the carpet, she gasped. She quickly ran to the linen closet, grabbed a towel, wet it, and began to wipe it up. The more she wiped, the worse the stains became. In desperation, she covered the stain with a small carpet. She knew this was a dumb idea but could not come up with anything else.

When her mother arrived home, as always, she marched around the house checking to see if everything was in its place. The mother noticed the dishes in the sink, the towel with the nacho cheese, salsa, and bits of chip sticking out of the hamper in the hall, the small carpet on the family room floor, and her daughter nervously lying on the couch. She calmly walked over to the small carpet, lifted it, and gasped. The mother looked at her daughter sternly and whispered, "I told you to be careful. This house is full of your clumsiness." Then she rattled off a long list of the daughter's mistakes and sent her to her room. In response, the daughter sprang up and screamed, "This is all your fault. Everybody has to be perfect around here. I'm sick of it! I'm sorry, sorry, sorry! There! Does that make you happy?" As she left the room, her mother yelled, "I have standards!" From that time forward, it became one battle after another. When she was finished, she slumped in the chair sobbing, "I can't ever please you. I'm such a screw up."

This ended the session. In the next one, mom defended herself. After some time discussing the importance of not keeping records, the mother stared blankly at her daughter. Then with tears in her eyes, she responded, "That must have been horrible growing up and feeling like you can never please me. I love you! I am so proud of you and who you have become. I am so sorry for bringing up all those past mistakes." After this, we began the restoration process. The mother had seen the importance of not keeping records.

Chapter 14

Restore Through Action

Once the transgressions are forgiven by both parties, it becomes time to begin the real restoration process to rebuild the relationship. Sometimes, it can be brought to the same level as it was before the incident. At other times, it returns to a lower level. Sometimes, it can actually be brought to a higher level of functioning with real effort on both sides. It depends on the effort of all involved as the Holy Spirit pours forth power into their lives.

A Typical Scenario

Have you ever had or heard a conversation with a spouse, sibling, or friend that went something like this? You say, "Hi! Well, today I finally worked things out with my mom. After all these years of struggle, I finally confronted her about all the things that she did in my childhood which were so hard on me. I was as gentle as possible without holding anything back. She apologized. Now I feel this huge burden lifted off of me, but I don't feel closer to her. I thought for sure things would feel different between us, but I still feel very little love for her when she is around."

If this were a scene from a movie, or a verse from a song, or chapter in a romance novel, then all the feelings would come flooding back. Then we would go off into the sunset and live happily ever after. This is pure fantasy and does not work that way in real human relationships. Neither is the opposite true. Once you have offended someone in a certain way, the feelings do not necessarily have to remain forever.

The person can get over what happened and the relationship can be restored. The past can be overcome. Getting "stuck in the past" may create a great dramatic moment in a movie, song, or story but never has to come true. Instead, any kind of relationship can be rebuilt if both parties desire it and will make the effort.

A Scriptural Principle

We now come to the final step in this important process of forgiveness and reconciliation. The fourteenth principle is "we must restore the relationship through words and actions and allow the feelings to follow." In Galatians 6:1, Paul explains this important concept when he exhorts the saints in Galatia, "Brothers, even if a man is caught in some fault, you who are spiritual must restore such a one in a spirit of gentleness." These "brothers" Paul refers to could be sinning against us.

What do we do with these brothers who sin? We ought to "restore" them. Here Paul is saying that as Christians, when we see someone caught in a sin, those who are spiritual should "restore" the person. The word translated "restore" not only encompasses restoration with God but all others who have been transgressed. In the apostle's context, the restorer is a Christian who sees a believer in sin. Yet, there are actually two other people who also might restore. These are the two people involved in a relationship that has gone awry: the one transgressed or the transgressor. This might occur after they have reconciled with the Lord God and now desire to reconcile with the other. In any of these three cases, there has been a transgression, and a restoration is obviously warranted. This restoration must always begin with the Lord God first. After this restoration takes place, the person we have transgressed should be addressed.

146

A Biblical Explanation

The next step in this forgiveness process is to restore. Sin destroys relationships and the Lord God desires for them to be restored. The Greek word translated "restore" means "to render fit, sound, or complete; to mend or repair what has been broken; to equip or prepare someone for something; to complete." In this context, it means to mend or repair what was broken. The word is used of a physically broken fishing net. In Mark 1:19 and Matthew 4:21, when Jesus called James and John into ministry with Him, they were in the process of "mending" their fishing nets. They were removing the holes in their net that would allow the fish to fall through. In 1 Corinthians 1:10 the Greek word is used of Christians being "complete" in the same mind and judgment. They are not to have any holes in their unity. The disagreement had to be mended, so all agreed.

The Lord Jesus gives us several steps we can take in the mending process in Revelation. In His vision, Jesus directs the apostle John to send seven letters to seven churches. In His letter to Ephesus, He begins with a description of their strengths as a church. In Revelation 2:1-3, Jesus comments, "I know your works, and your toil and perseverance, and that you can't tolerate evil men, and have tested those who call themselves apostles, and they are not, and found them false. You have perseverance and have endured for my name's sake and have not grown weary." Notice, the Lord Jesus began with a complement. He listed the things that He most appreciated about them and their relationship to Him. This is step one. We should engage in words that complement the person we are attempting to reconcile with. Words that focus on their true strengths are so important as we begin.

Then the Lord Jesus mentions their exact transgressions. In Revelation 2:4, He admonishes, "But I have this against you, that you left your first love." The Lord obviously means Himself. They had gotten so caught up in the battle that they had forgotten who they were battling for. In a relational sense, they had begun taking the Lord Jesus for granted. In the first part of Revelation 2:5, He describes what they must do, "Remember therefore from where you have fallen." Jesus asked them to think back and remember the time before they had fallen into their broken relationship. Why? They need to remind themselves of how good it was and how far they were from it. This is step two.

Then, at the end of verse 5, the Lord Jesus asks them to repent. This we have already discussed. After this, Christ commanded them to go and "do the first works or deeds" they had done from the beginning with Him. They must return to the beginning actions. It is these deeds that should take place again. The focus is not on the actions of love one does in the middle of a relationship, but the ones done at the beginning. This is a huge difference. Restoration requires the new, fresh, more intense deeds one does as a relationship is beginning to blossom. These are the actions that quickly build relationships. Step three is to do the beginning deeds. Notice, the Ephesians had to mend their relationship with their actions. He does not appeal to their feelings. Our mind decides what is right; then our actions follow next. Once the actions have commenced, the feelings will follow them.

Now, what were these initial actions that the church did? They are the same actions and deeds every church did when it was established. In Acts 2:42, Luke describes them in these words, "They continued steadfastly in the apostles' teaching and fellowship, in the breaking of bread [communion], and prayer." They were praying (talking to God) and reading His Word (letting Him talk to them). The saints were receiving communion (remembering Jesus Christ's great sacrifice with thanksgiving) and fellowshipping with others (serving and supporting the saints in words and deeds). Apply this to our human relationships now. Our first deeds would be to talk with the people who need restoration and really listen to them. This is the word and prayer. We should look at their good qualities and the great relationship we had with them in the past and be grateful for them. This is like communion. Then, we should serve them and support them with words and deeds of kindness. Finally, we should be around people who would encourage our relationships. This is what the Bible calls fellowship.

Whenever we take the time to have a conversation with, listen to, complement, show appreciation and gratitude, or serve those we have offended or have offended us, we mend a small hole in the relationship net. We must keep doing this until all the holes are mended, and the relationship is whole again. We should realize that this will also take to mend. Does it not take some time to mend a fishing net? These nets were large and were spread out on the rocks and mended carefully. Why? They could not afford for the net to break again.

It does not matter what their response is when we begin the mending process, nor does it matter what our feelings are. We should keep doing the many beginning deeds of love and expect the previous feelings to return. Normally, this will be to their previous level. If we continue to do these deeds, then we may actually increase the feelings and bring them to a higher level. If the feelings do not return and the deeds are being done with good intentions, then it is time to pray for divine intervention on both our parts. Of course, with Christians the Lord expects effort on both sides which makes a real difference. Unfortunately, this does not always happen. If we have a true open heart and the willingness to to exert the effort that is necessary, then we must rely on the Holy Spirit to do the rest.

Who should begin this restoration process? The answer is found in Galatians 6:1 where Paul indicates that it is "the one who is spiritual" who starts the process. I always say, "First one filled with the Spirit has to take the first action." The first one in the relationship who is filled with the fruits of the Spirit begins the restoration (Galatians 5:22-23). The Lord also expects the more mature Christian to take the lead if needed. If we have a broken relationship and we have been a believer longer, then we need to go. This principle should also involve the many relationships we have with those who are unsaved. If we have a broken relationship with a non-believer, then we are the spiritual one. We need to take the first step. It does not matter who started it, or whose fault it is, once we become "spiritual," we should seek to restore the relationship with all the parties involved.

An Ancient Portrait

In Genesis, Moses described a sibling relationship which had been broken for over twenty years. It had been between twin brothers who would not speak to each other because of one's deceit and the other's spite. Yet, twenty years later God would set up a series of circumstances that would force a reconciliation between these two brothers. These two were Jacob and Esau and the reconciliation occurs in Genesis 32-34. Though Jacob and Esau were twins, since Esau was born first, he stood to inherit two-thirds of all that His father Isaac owned. Yet, Esau cared little about it. One day Esau was famished, so his twin brother Jacob offered him a bowl of lentil soup in exchange for his inheritance. Foolishly, Esau agreed. Later, Jacob impersonated his brother before an almost blind father by putting animal skins on his arms to also steal his blessing. This he did and left nothing but a curse for his older brother. Esau had had enough. He swore that he would kill Jacob as soon as his father had died. Once his mother found out, she sent Jacob to her brother Laban's family for protection. Then his twin brother Esau then left the household in disgust.

During the course of those twenty years, the both of them prospered financially and materially. They grew very large families and had households full of servants. Finally, it was time for Jacob to depart from his uncle's land and move back to his father's territory. To do this, he had to travel through Esau's land which was extensive. There was no way around it. He wanted to avoid a confrontation, but God's way has always been reconciliation and restoration, if at all possible. So, in God's providence, Jacob had to cross the land. Don't we do that? A holiday arrives, and we do everything we can in order to avoid a face-to-face meeting. We might even be in the same room but never speak to one another. The Lord God never acts this way towards us and does not expect us to act this way towards any others. Instead, He expects us to restore relationships through action.

So, Jacob took action. He set up camp near his property and devised plans for their reconciliation. Jacob selected gifts of his herds and flocks of animals for Esau: goats, sheep, camels, colts, cows, bulls, and donkeys. He divided them up into three groups according to their herds and flocks and sent a messenger ahead of them in each group. On three different occasions, Esau would be greeted with gifts of reconciliation. Each time, his brother Esau was addressed as "Lord Esau" and was told that Jacob was behind them hoping that these gifts would calm and satisfy him, so he would accept Jacob when they met face to face. After the third set of gifts, the time had arrived.

Jacob spent the last night before his encounter wrestling with an angel. Here God reiterated His covenant with Jacob and changed his name to Israel which would become the name of the nation in his loins. God assured Jacob that he did not have to worry about Esau because the Lord would protect him. The next day, Esau arrived. Jacob bowed to the ground seven times as he was approaching his twin brother. Here he was honoring him and demonstrating submission and sorrow over what he had done. This clearly indicated that Jacob desired reconciliation. Suddenly, Esau began to run toward Jacob. Would he kill him or embrace him? He grabbed him, hugged him, fell on his neck, and kissed him on the cheek. He saw the women and children who were with him and immediately inquired as to who they were. Then both his wives and their families bowed down. Esau asked why they had all come. Jacob replied that he wanted to find favor in Esau's sight and travel through his land on his way home. The implication was crystal clear he wanted to restore their relationship.

Esau then did something that could only have occurred through the providence of God. He declared that he did not need his gifts because God had provided for him. Then Jacob insisted that he keep them because he saw in Esau the face of God. God was at work because Esau had welcomed him favorably. Finally, his brother Esau accepted the gifts. Then, Esau suggested that they journey through his land together, and Esau would travel ahead of him. Jacob had to refuse because the herds and flocks had to travel at their own pace. Esau then suggested that he leave some of his men with him to assist in the journey. Again, Jacob refused. He did not feel the need, and so Esau departed. Then, Jacob followed at his own pace. The two brothers worked things out.

I do not think we see all of God's steps of reconciliation in this story because Jacob and Esau were never very close as brothers. Mom and dad had seen to that through their acts of favoritism. Also, they were very different people. The story does accent some of the most important points. Jacob did restore the relationship through his actions. There was gift giving and signs of respect. They stumbled over each other in their recognition of God's blessing upon each of them. Esau offered support for Jacob's journey through his land. They parted as reconciled brothers. This is all they desired. They both did what was right. They restored what they had through actions and allowed their feelings to follow. This is all God requires.

A Modern Anecdote

One day, a set of adult triplets (two men and a woman) walked into my office and described how distraught they were over the deteriorating relationships among themselves and their families. This occurred after their mother became completely incapacitated from a stroke. Since their father had passed away, they decided to allow their mother to stay in the family home with a live-in nurse. During this critical time, they each visited her separately or the two brothers would see her together but never the three of them. Then she passed away. When they met and began discussing funeral arrangements, it turned into an argument. This argument led to accusations concerning the future of their family home, furnishings, and savings. Once they reached an impasse, the sister went to complain to her pastor who referred them to me.

As the discussion began, it was not long before the two brothers were accusing the sister of trying to control and dominate them; in return, she was accusing them of ganging up against her. It was almost as if they were about twelve years old arguing over who would get the last piece of pie. It became very obvious that they had grown up in constant conflict. I asked them to describe their mother's interactions with them. They all agreed that their mother was a strong and domineering woman whose solution to every problem was simply shouting, "Stop fighting and go to your rooms." She never once took the time to discover what they may have been arguing about. This action led to a great amount of conflict occurring behind their mother's back. They began to learn very quickly to deal with things themselves which often led to many instances of physical confrontation. Since the sister always had her own room and she was a girl, the battle lines were easily drawn. The two boys constantly challenged the sister or vice versa. It would get so chaotic at times that things around the house would be broken. When their mother would demand an explanation, all three would stick together and claim that they had no idea what she was talking about.

This fighting and arguing continued until the sister got married and then moved out of the house. Then the mother would have monthly family dinners at her house, and she would accept no excuse for not attending. Either the three of them alone, with their spouses, or with their children would sit there as if everything were fine. When they left, the two brothers would not speak to their sister again until a holiday or these cold, bitter family dinners occurred. When their mother passed away, the pretense was over, the anger and bitterness poured forth, and the fighting once again began.

I explained to them that I could and would help facilitate the decisions that had to be made concerning the mother's funeral, but I would like to meet with them afterward. They had some serious relationship problems and needed to work these out for the sake of their children and their children's children. Often a dominant mother with children who have difficulty getting along will usually separate after her death. Thereafter, the aunts and uncles, nieces and nephews, and cousins will no longer interact with one another. Multiply that by several generations, and this family no longer exists.

Though they were hesitant to act, everyone agreed when the children were mentioned. Once the funeral was over, they made an appointment to see me. It required some time to go through the reconciliation process, but it was well worth it. Once they had forgiven each other, we developed a strategy for them to restore their relationships through action. Then plans were created to strengthen all the various relationships among their families. Once these actions began, new feelings of love toward one another also began.

Conclusion

As we conclude this book, I would like to leave us with some final thoughts about our God of forgiveness and what His Son did on the cross for us. First, if we understand the full extent of what was wrought for us on that cursed tree in order to forgive us, it will become so much easier to do the same thing for others. Second, if you read this entire book and realized that you do not understand salvation or have never received Christ as Lord and Savior, then I would like to provide that opportunity. Please do not skip this section; it may be the most important in your life.

From all outward appearances, humans seem "good" and attempt to live decent lives. This is man's concept of himself. This is not God's concept. The Almighty's view is that people all over the world and throughout the ages sin, sin, and sin again (Romans 3:23). This is a terrible and utterly destructive condition. Yet, they have ramifications that are far worse. These sins condemn us to everlasting divine retribution.

Though described briefly in the Old Testament, the Lord Jesus Christ clearly announced and proclaimed the future punishment to come. Contrary to popular belief, Jesus did not only speak of love, grace, and mercy, He also spoke of the coming judgment for sin. He declared that the judgment of sin would be everlasting punishment in a place He called "Hell." The Lord portrayed this place as an eternal inferno (Matthew 18:8) where there would be the weeping (from the sorrow) and gnashing of teeth (from the agony and anguish of suffering) continually into eternity (Matthew 8:12; 13:42, 50; 22:13; 24:51; 25:30; Luke 13:28).

Why must people face this horrific punishment? Though God is a God of love, grace, and mercy, He is also a God of great holiness, righteousness, and justice (Psalm 89:14,18). These attributes are just as much a part of His divine nature as His love, grace, and mercy. You have broken God's law as we all have, and the penalty must be paid. This began with the first man Adam (Genesis 3:1-7). When this occurred, His love, grace, and mercy surfaced, and a provision was made. Someone else would have to take man's place and pay the penalty. Someone who had never transgressed Him, who would never deserve punishment, and would fulfill all of God's Laws, would be substituted in man's place. This was the Son of God, Jesus Christ.

As the God-Man, He would pay the penalty for our sins in His death on the cross. Once done, the Lord God made only one provision for people to appropriate what His Son had done on the cross for them. This provision is receiving Jesus Christ as Savior and Lord. Though I cannot possibly share with you this good news in the confines of this book, I would love for you to consider purchasing my book entitled, *Finding The Light: The Kingdom of Heaven and How To Enter It*. It can be found for sale on Amazon.com. It is inexpensive and contains the full gospel message for your consideration. This message is so important and extensive that it cannot adequately be contained in a few pages at the end of a book.

If you are a believer, you must go out into the world and forgive as you are forgiven. These principles are to be lived and shared with others. You now have the tools to make your relationships last a lifetime. Go live them out and share them with others!

ABOUT THE AUTHOR

Dr. Donald Jones is currently a Christian Pastoral Counselor with thirty-eight years of experience in the fields of pastoral ministry, public education, and Christian counseling. He carries degrees and certificates from four major universities and from a variety of educational institutions. He has been a professor of Languages and Bible, a television commentator, and a featured speaker at a variety of events and seminars at churches, schools, and other organizations across the United States. He is a member in good standing of several secular and Christian professional organizations. Dr. Jones has been a published author since 1976. For further information view his website at www.donjonesphd.com.

www.ingramcontent.com/pod-product-compliance
Lightning Source LLC
La Vergne TN
LVHW011330080426
835513LV00006B/275

* 9 7 8 0 6 9 2 7 4 1 2 3 8 *